HOW TO ASK FOR AND GET WHAT YOU WANT

HOW TO ASK FOR AND GET WHAT YOU WANT

Commonsense Tips That Work

Catherine DePino

ROWMAN & LITTLEFIELD
Lanham • Boulder • New York • London

Published by Rowman & Littlefield
An imprint of The Rowman & Littlefield Publishing Group, Inc.
4501 Forbes Boulevard, Suite 200, Lanham, Maryland 20706
www.rowman.com

6 Tinworth Street, London SE11 5AL, United Kingdom

British Library Cataloguing in Publication Information Available

Library of Congress Cataloging-in-Publication Data

Names: DePino, Catherine, author.
Title: How to ask for and get what you want : commonsense tips that work / Catherine DePino.
Description: Lanham : Rowman & Littlefield Publishing Group, 2020. | Includes bibliographical references. | Summary: "This book that employs mindfulness principles to address how to ask and receive in different situations, such as dealing with partners, children, and businesses"— Provided by publisher.
Identifiers: LCCN 2020003693 (print) | LCCN 2020003694 (ebook) | ISBN 9781475857191 (cloth) | ISBN 9781475857207 (epub)
Subjects: LCSH: Mindfulness (Psychology) | Negotiation. | Self-help techniques.
Classification: LCC BF637.M56 D47 2020 (print) | LCC BF637.M56 (ebook) | DDC 158.2—dc23
LC record available at https://lccn.loc.gov/2020003693
LC ebook record available at https://lccn.loc.gov/2020003694

For my grandson, Cole Andrew: You light up our lives with your winning ways and magical smile. May you always find joy in every day. Love, Nonna

Ask and it will be given to you; seek and you shall find; knock and the door will be opened to you.
—Matthew 7:7, from the New International Version of the Bible

CONTENTS

ACKNOWLEDGMENTS

I'd like to thank Carlie Wall, managing editor, for her competence and kindness, and Dr. Tom Koerner, vice president and editorial director, for his support and encouragement. I am grateful to Catherine Herman, an exemplary editorial assistant in production, for her expertise, willingness to help, and caring ways. I appreciate my daughter Shayna DePino Kudgis's expertise as a school counselor for the book's education section. Thanks to my husband, Dr. Andrew DePino, who served on the local school board, for information in the education section about school boards.

INTRODUCTION

How to Use This Book

We've all experienced frustration asking for and getting what we want. It plays out regularly with our partners, kids, employers, and businesses we patronize. Sometimes we don't bother to ask for what we want, even when it's perfectly reasonable, thinking it will create hard feelings or spark an argument. Often, it's because we don't think we can succeed in getting what we want. But nothing could be further from the truth.

This book will help you learn how to ask for what you want and get good results. It teaches you how to stay in the game by using the right words. It also shows you how to build rapport by using positive body language. The more you know about what makes people operate as they do, the better chance you have of helping them see things your way.

I've based the material in this book upon my years of experience as a tough cookie mom/teacher/grandmom who knows what she wants and doesn't hesitate to ask for it. Most of the time, I succeed, and I want you to also. That's why I wrote this book.

The most important aspect to negotiating anything is getting the other person on your side. That means the person you're asking has to like and respect you enough to do what you want. When I taught high school, I learned quickly that if I wanted students to learn and cooperate, I had to find a way to get them to like and trust me.

If they found me boring or bossy, it would put a damper on establishing rapport with them so they'd be more likely to succeed in school and love learning. I had to show them that I was in control and command so they would see me as strong and assertive rather than a pushover. That's what you have to do to get people to cooperate and give you what you want.

I'm not saying it's easy. It's more like a tightrope walk, a matter of balance, where people have to both like and respect you at the same time. I'll show you how to get people on your side to help you get what you want.

In many cases, people go on living with issues they could have easily remedied by asking a partner, child, boss, or company to grant them what they want by using simple yet magic words you'll find in chapter 1. It's important to talk so people listen if you want to get what you're seeking. This chapter shows how to speak assertively, use body language, and build rapport to your advantage so you'll have the best chance of getting what you want. Finally, if you show curiosity about people, you'll understand them better and will have a better chance of their granting your wishes.

Negotiating with someone on the phone often proves more challenging than talking in person because you can't read the verbal cues or body language the other person projects. Your chances of getting what you want rest mainly on what you say and how the other person responds, so phone conversations often present more challenges than face-to-face encounters. See chapter 2 for tips about how to request things on the phone and when it's helpful to go to a higher level for help. When you're asking for something on the phone, be willing to go to the next level if you're not satisfied with the first person you encounter.

It's sometimes harder to ask and receive from a partner than with others because you're closely connected. That's the scope of chapter 3. It's important to know when and how to ask to get the results you want. If you follow the advice in chapter 3, it can help your partner become more involved with the kids by providing him with more opportunities to bond with them. Besides dealing with relationship issues between you, your partner, and your children, chapter 3 addresses asking for and getting the spiritual and physical intimacy that's important to your relationship. Along with all the other chapters, this one also shows how practicing mindfulness can enhance family relationships.

Consider this example with your teenage son: he talks back, balks at doing homework, and responds to your suggestions with grunts, groans, and guffaws. Does this sound familiar? Discover ideas for getting your child to listen and respond to your requests in chapter 4. This chapter also emphasizes the importance of standing by what you say when dealing with your kids. At the same time, it helps to cut your children some slack when they will benefit by that approach. Flexibility in child-raising helps immeasurably. Most important, encourage your children to make their own decisions, but stay close by to guide them.

You'll find ideas about how to strike good deals with home services, restaurants, cars, and vacation rentals in chapter 5. Moreover, you'll get advice about how to negotiate when your TV/internet bundle bill is due. Every time spring rolls around, the cable company raises it. That makes you think of switching to another company you dislike more because of its low-speed internet and lack of top-quality free movies.

You also wonder if you can live without NFL, NBA, cable news, free movies, and your other favorites. You put off calling, but you know you'll have to haggle over your bill eventually if you want to make a last-ditch effort to stay with the company. Check out time-tested ways of negotiating with companies to get results.

Chapter 6 gives you practical tips about how to address problems with companies that give you inferior services or products. This chapter also addresses what to do when you come to an impasse with a service company. Additionally, this chapter helps you fix a problem with an online store. It also informs you about what your state representative can do to help you with local and national issues that affect your everyday life. If you need to ask a company about a defective product, this chapter will help you. How and when to contact a company's corporate office is another feature of chapter 6.

Getting a family member or friend to accept your point of view, even if they don't embrace it, can create drama and conflicts. Worse, it can cool or destroy friendships. Chapter 7 helps you, your family, and friends disagree in peaceful, noncombative ways.

Chapter 8 helps you create your best impression in job interviews from what to say to how to dress. It also gives you helpful sample questions to guide your preparation for your interview. Moreover, you'll learn how to use body language to its best advantage when you're applying for a job. Finally, you'll learn a winning formula for asking the perfect closing question to conclude a successful interview.

Sometimes you face challenges getting along with your employer so you can work harmoniously yet maintain your integrity and belief in handling things in the best way possible, even when it conflicts with your boss's ideas. Possibly, you're up for a promotion and feel that your boss doesn't see you as a viable candidate. How can you ask for and get what you want at work? Chapter 9 gives ideas for dealing with work-related problems, such as getting a coworker to stop bothering you and staving off workplace bullies. You'll also get helpful pointers about how to ask for a raise.

Chapter 10 addresses how to ask for what you want and get it in the educational arena. I've included this information because Rowman & Littlefield relates to the educational arena. In addition to addressing how educators can best get their needs met by school administrators, it speaks to the concerns of parents and students in navigating the educational system to get good results. This chapter also helps parents obtain their school board's help when they need it.

In chapter 11 you'll find some commonly asked questions that deal with topics you may find difficult to ask for and address. You'll also find tips on how to say no when someone asks for something you don't want to give.

As a thank you for reading this book, you'll also find a recipe for lemon chiffon dessert. I hope you get everything you ask for by following these commonsense tips. I think you'll find the process both fun and user friendly.

Most of the advice in this book employs mindfulness techniques. The mindfulness movement brought to America by Jon Kabat-Zinn via the teachings of Thich Nhat Hanh, Zen master and global spiritual leader, helps people live in the moment, speak more effectively to one another, and settle problems peacefully. Many schools incorporate mindfulness in their curricula to cut down on bullying and confrontations.

Similarly, when you use the ideas in this book, you'll find it easier to come to a peaceful resolution with others and get what you're asking for without acting pushy or passive.

Mindfulness promotes talking to people as you'd want them to talk to you in an assertive, yet kind, manner. You want them to know exactly where you stand and what you want. They, in turn, want you to listen to what they have to say and to respond courteously and patiently.

I suggest that you read the entire book first so that you can learn all the different tips and decide which ones to apply to your individual issues to maximize your success in getting what you want. After you complete the book, go back and look at chapters that relate to your situations as the need arises. Apply the tips you learn here to your unique issues, and modify them with your own personal communication style. Write to me on my website or my author Facebook page to tell me how the techniques worked for you.

Happy asking and receiving!

Note to reader: The author varies the use of he and she in the interest of maintaining inclusive language.

I

USE THESE TECHNIQUES TO GET WHAT YOU WANT

TALK SO PEOPLE LISTEN

Showing your best self and "making nice" is always the best approach in asking for what you want. It doesn't mean being a "kiss-up" that others can easily see through when they realize you're trying to weasel something out of them. Here's the bottom line: showing genuine sincerity and politeness goes a long way in helping you establish rapport with the person on the giving end.

Once you set the stage for asking, state exactly what you're seeking without using unnecessary words. That means you need to speak strongly and directly. If you're talking with a friend or family member, start the conversation with assertive words and phrases like these: "I need [or I'd like] to talk with you about [whatever it is you're asking for]. Let's set a time that's good for both of us." Include the last sentence because the longer you put off the discussion, the harder it becomes to reach your goal.

Avoid passive communication that will make you appear wimpy and weak. Here's an example: "When you have time, would you be willing to talk about something that's been on my mind?" By the time you've made your request, the other person is probably rolling her eyes, watching the clock, thinking, "I have more important things to do. Whatever you want to talk to me about can wait."

On the other hand, avoid aggressive talk, such as "I've had it with you. We're going to talk about this now." Nobody likes to be lectured or bullied. Talk with others as you'd want them to talk to you. People value those who speak honestly and say exactly what's on their minds without mincing any words, but it's important to show respect and courtesy for the person you're asking if you want to get him on your side. If you talk using mindfulness principles, you'll get results. Talking assertively rather than passively or aggressively is a good way to start. People will know where you stand and will respect you when you negotiate.

Use "magic words" to frame your request. Pepper your conversation with "please," "thank you," "I appreciate your help," and other polite expressions. Beyond that, consider using time-tested phrases like this: "I'm hoping you can help me so that we can figure out how to solve the problem."

These expressions work well with companies whether you're negotiating contracts or registering a complaint. Aggressive speech such as "What's up with that, you [nasty name]?" never works. Taking the passive, negative route and saying, "I don't know how I'm going to get this problem resolved. I don't know if anyone can fix it" proves equally ineffective.

When you're trying to get a child to cooperate, and see she's upset, bend to her level, look at her calmly, and say, "What can I do to help?" or "What would it take for you to feel better?" Use these questions with people of all ages. They show you're on their side and will help them calm down and put things in perspective. Back up your words with eye contact and body language. Also, consider that you, more than anyone, know the person you're dealing with in your inner circle of family and friends. You know what words to use to entice her to listen and respond. Think of what has worked for you in the past, and use it as part of your asking/receiving repertoire.

If one approach doesn't get you what you want, delete it from your script, and brainstorm with yourself until you find a more promising technique. Self-talk is an effective mindfulness technique you can use in many circumstances to help you find the right words. It means talking to yourself as you would a trusted friend or family member to help you find an answer. Experiment with different possibilities to help you find the right approach, and you'll discover the solution that's right for you.

BUILD RAPPORT WITH EYE CONTACT AND BODY LANGUAGE

If you want to make what you're requesting happen, build rapport with the person you're asking. Use these tips when you're talking in person. First, make it a point to use good eye contact to help build rapport. Naturally, you don't want to stare the person down; you know how intimidating that can be. Instead, look at him like you're truly interested in what he has to say.

Make sure he knows that you value his opinion, even if differs from yours. If you're talking to your partner or your child, you already know what works in getting their attention and what makes them avoid listening to you. Timing plays a part in getting good results. Avoid asking for something when the person you're talking to seems preoccupied or out of sorts.

Be aware of body language, how people use their bodies to emphasize certain points by showing approval for some ideas and displeasure for others. Observe how your friends, family, and acquaintances use body language to get their messages across. What do you think they're saying with their body language and gestures when they speak or respond to something you say?

Using body language effectively is one of the best ways to build rapport with another person as you make your request. Boost your message by using body language, so that people both hear and see what you're saying. The more senses you use in making your request, the more likely the person will respond positively. Above all, listen and give her your full attention by responding to specific things she says with speech and implies with body language. That way, she'll be aware you're listening and understand her ideas, whether or not you agree. When someone believes you're listening, she'll be more likely to reciprocate.

Is how the people you talk with use body language consistent with their message, or are they trying to tell you something completely different from what their words imply? If their body language goes along with their message, it's a good indicator that you can trust its reliability. If not, you may want to act curious and ask questions to help you understand what they they're trying to say. Being curious is one of the hallmarks of mindfulness, and it can shed light on any situation if you ask the right questions.

Here's an example of body language that's consistent with what a person says—in this case, your child's teacher. You're appealing to your child's high school teacher to reconsider giving your son a poor English grade. Your son added up his grades and they came to a C–, but he received a D. During a parent-teacher conference, the teacher crossed his arms and said, "I always double-check my grades, but I'll look over your son's grades again. I'll call you if I find there's any change in the final grade."

Don't hold your breath waiting for him to call. Most people know that crossed arms mean resistance. By observing the teacher's body language, you'll probably deduce that the teacher isn't going change your son's grade.

Conversely, picture the teacher making eye contact with you, nodding, and assuming an open, relaxed pose as you make your request to reconsider his grade. You can assume he will reconsider the original grade and may possibly change it if all the figures add up.

It pays to be acutely aware of body language when you're asking someone to consider your appeal. Let it guide you when you choose your words to ask for what you want. A frown, a raised eyebrow, or a hand covering the mouth (which may mean the listener doubts your words) can often act as a prompt to change your tactic in negotiating. On the other hand, if the person you're trying to convince leans in slightly toward you and assumes a relaxed posture, it probably means he's more receptive to listening to you.

Test the reliability of body language by being curious and observing whether a person uses body language consistently when expressing opinions about the issues you're discussing. Ask yourself if the body language appears random when it accompanies certain words or if it relates directly to the speaker's words. It's often easier to determine the congruency between a message and body language when talking with family and friends since you spend more time with them than with acquaintances or people you don't know.

MIRROR BODY LANGUAGE TO ENHANCE RAPPORT

Mirroring body language is a good way to enhance rapport to get what you want. Mirroring means imitating people's body language to show that you're like them. When imitating body language, do it subtly, rather than boldly, giving it your own variations, so it doesn't look fake or comical. People feel comfortable toward those who resemble them in speech and gestures. When you assume the style of others in speech and body language, you show you're like them. This gives them the message that you think positively about them, and that means they'll be more likely to listen and grant your request.

Mirroring body language can strengthen or dampen your message as it can with the person receiving your message. For example, if an employer with whom you're trying to score points leans toward you when speaking, do the same. You can mirror the way she sits, stands, and uses her hands in conversation. Make your gestures differ slightly from hers so that what you're doing doesn't look too obvious.

Avoid negative body language, even if the other person uses it, or it may backfire. Steepling (putting your fingers together, sometimes accompanied by leaning back in your chair) may give the impression of superiority and arrogance although sometimes it simply indicates confidence. You'll be able to determine what it represents by listening to a person's speech and by observing his other body language to figure out his intentions.

Think about how your body language affects the person you're trying to impress. She may perceive looking away or to the side, instead of directly at her, as a lack of interest in what she's saying. Crossing your arms may mean you're not open to what she says. If the person you're trying to convince uses gestures you perceive as negative, take the cue seriously and use a different approach to make your request.

You can also try to imitate the speaking style of the person you want to engage. For example, if an employer tends to talk informally and use basic vocabulary, mimic that language style, rather than using grad school words and complex sentence structures. If he uses an advanced vocabulary and speaks more formally, use a similar vocabulary so that he feels more comfortable relating to your message. You want to sound like the person you're addressing but not so much like him that you sound like you're trying to ingratiate yourself with him by imitating him.

SPEAK TO ENHANCE YOUR MESSAGE

Besides using body language and speech to enhance rapport, model the tone of the person you're asking. If she speaks with expression, sound animated; if she's more businesslike and formal, use that tone. Stay on the person's tone level to get the most mileage out of your conversation.

When asking for something, use strong statements so listeners know exactly where you stand. Avoid passive linking verbs (any part of the verb *to be*, such as *am*, *is*, *are*, *was*, and *were*). Instead, use vibrant, specific verbs and nouns to reinforce your message. For example, saying, "I was disappointed by the frozen mac and cheese I bought from your company" uses *was*, a weak linking verb. It also doesn't state a specific request for what you want from the company.

"The frozen mac and cheese from your company disappointed me. Please send me a refund for the product I bought at my local Giant Supermarket" states your complaint more directly. Pump up your request by using strong action verbs and by providing specific detail about what you want.

Here's an example of using a general noun versus a specific one in stating your dissatisfaction with a product; in this case, hairspray: "My hair is clumpy and sticky after using your hairspray" uses the linking verb *is* and states the problem in a general way. It's more helpful to say, "Your 'Super Spray for Curly Hair' makes my hair straight and flyaway, the opposite of what the product promises in your advertising."

Instead, state the exact name of the product and provide details about what you want from the company like this: "Please send me a refund of $15 to cover the cost of the product I purchased at 'Make-Up Galore' in Naples, Florida." Specific nouns and verbs, along with details about what you're asking from the company, get better results than general ones.

Here's another example of lackluster speech versus lively, specific speech. Listen to these two ways of saying the same thing: "I'm upset about the inferior stand mixer your company makes. It's a piece of junk" versus "I need you to send a replacement immediately for the Deluxe Stand Mixer, Model 14. It failed to work properly from day one."

The first statement lacks details and sounds vague, while the second states the message strongly and directly. When you say what you mean and mean what you say to a company, a family member, or friend, you'll usually get the results you want.

Steer clear of verbal tics, certain words and sounds, such as *like, just, um, ah*, and *you know*. Verbal tics give the impression that you're fumbling for what to say and may make the person you're addressing think you don't have a clear message.

Most of us have verbal tics we use frequently without knowing it. Think of the ones you use, and be aware of them when you're talking so that people perceive you as strong and assertive rather than weak and indecisive. If you're not sure you have verbal tics, ask a friend or family member who's honest enough to tell you if you use them and what they are. Verbal tics and vague expressions put a damper on reaching your goal of getting what you want.

When you're considering how to talk to others so you come across well in making your request, you'll also want to avoid a way of speaking called *vocal fry*. Some people think they sound more authoritative if they speak this way. A few newscasters and public figures use vocal fry when they lower their voices to talk in a deep, throaty tone instead of sounding natural and relaxed. You can find examples of vocal fry on YouTube if you plug "vocal fry" into the search bar. Although many people associate vocal fry with the way women speak in order to sound assertive, some men also speak this way to sound more authoritative.

People who use vocal fry think they sound strong and assertive, but the person they're talking to may wonder if they're auditioning for a comedy act. Speaking like this or using other devices to sound like an inauthentic imitation of yourself will not advance your cause. Worse, it often backfires. Be yourself every time you ask for something. Getting what you want will prove much easier.

When asking for something, also avoid upspeak, which happens when you end a statement on an "up note" with a rising inflection so that it sounds like a question. Upspeak gives the impression that you don't have confidence in yourself or know what you're talking about. It doesn't help to sound this way, especially if you're asking for something. If you make a statement, say it with as much authority as you can muster without sounding aggressive.

Keep in mind that your tone, language usage, and the inflections and nuances in your voice can make or break you when you make a request. Be conscious of your speech patterns and body language at all times because they often impart a stronger message than your words.

BE CURIOUS ABOUT PEOPLE

Curiosity, a mindfulness trait, can help you reach your goal of getting what you want. Before you use any of the tips outlined here, it helps to be curious about the person you're dealing with, whether she's sitting in front of you or miles away, talking on the phone.

Ask yourself, "What makes this person who she is? How can I best reach out to her so she understands where I'm coming from and what I want? What will it take for her to understand my way of thinking?" Reviewing these questions helps you collect your thoughts and sort things out before you put your plan in place. Trust your curiosity and intuition to help you find the best plan of action for making the recipient of your request listen and respond.

THINK ABOUT HOW PEOPLE USE LANGUAGE

After preparing your plan for getting someone to see things your way and give you what you want, you're ready to refine your presentation. Here are some additional suggestions: besides using eye contact, positive body language, speaking effectively, and acting curious, be mindful of the way people use language.

All of us use pet phrases when we talk. Some of us use phrases that appeal to the sense of sight; others favor hearing, while some people tend to use words and phrases that deal with the sense of touch. Most of us use a combination of words and phrases that relate to different senses. However, one or two senses usually predominate in most people. Which words and phrases do you often use? Think about whether they relate to sight, hearing, or touch. Knowing this can help you see how you and others perceive the world.

If you see the world in a visual way, you may use words like "I see what you mean" or "Picture this." If you perceive things by using words and phrases related to hearing, you'll probably favor phrases like this: "I hear what you're saying" or "Before you say anything, I'd appreciate it if you'd hear me out." If you're more of a hands-on person, you're likely to use wording like "Are you getting a feel for what I'm saying?" or "Let's toss our ideas back and forth to see how we can agree."

Be curious. Listen to how the person you're negotiating with speaks. Maybe you've never noticed his pet phrases before. Once you're clear on how he uses language, try using similar, but not the same, words and phrases when you're asking for or negotiating something important to you. It's another way of building rapport to get the person on your side. Once you get him on your side, you set the stage for asking.

When you understand who you're dealing with and how he processes the world around him, you'll be able to plan the best individual strategy for asking so you'll be more likely to get what you want. Keep in mind that when you live with someone for a long time you may lose sight of the best way to reach that person when you're requesting something.

You're so used to thinking of a family member or close friend in a certain way that sometimes you don't take all facets of that person's personality into account when you request something. Also, people often change the way they react depending on the way they're feeling on a particular day. Take the time to be curious and ask yourself questions about how to best approach your spouse, child, or boss before you make your case. Go armed with a strategy that will bring you success.

You can also use this technique when negotiating a contract with a company, such as your cable provider, or a service provider, like a plumber or electrician, by spending a few minutes chatting rather than plunging right into the business of asking. Be curious when you talk to people, and you'll learn how to read them so you know how best to approach them when you need their help.

Whether you're dealing with a family member or a businessperson, you sometimes text or email, especially when you don't have time to talk in person or on the phone. Try mimicking the way the person you're negotiating with uses email, texting, or letter writing the way you imitate body language, gestures, and speech.

If the person you're corresponding with writes in short, pithy sentences, copy that. If she uses a fancy, flowery style, embellish your writing to make it sound more literary. Also, pay attention to the greeting and closing the person uses, and make yours similar. Is it *Yours truly, Kind regards* (always a good one), *Sincerely*, or *Best wishes (Best* for short)?

Be curious about what kind of vibe you get from the other person's email, text, or letter. Does it seem formal or more relaxed? If you're texting someone, does she use a lot of shortcuts, like *u* for *you*, or are all the words spelled out? People relate better to those who act like them, and that includes email, texting, or writing letters.

To summarize, before you ask for something, prepare in advance by getting to know about the person listening to your request. That means always being polite, using magic words, building rapport with good eye contact and body language, and considering the other person's view of the world and appealing to it.

INSTANT REVIEW

Chapter 1: Use These Techniques to Get What You Want

- Show your best self.
- Talk so people listen.
- Speak assertively.
- Use "magic words."
- Build rapport.
- Mirror positive body language.
- Speak to enhance your message.
- Be curious about people.
- Think about how people use language.

2

GET RESULTS ON THE PHONE

BE POSITIVE

If you're not requesting something in person as you would in the case of a family member, employer, or service provider, you can employ many of the same techniques on the phone, such as showing politeness, speaking assertively, and using the right words.

If you're talking on the phone and the person you're talking to seems pressed for time, which often happens in both small and corporate business, arm yourself with additional techniques. Often, you won't have time to rehearse your script or be curious about the person to whom you're speaking so that you can figure out an effective way to approach him when making your request.

Even though you can't see the face behind the voice, you can do something to promote your cause to get the person on your side. Make a strong effort to be positive, especially at the beginning of the conversation. A testy, aggressive attitude will turn off the person you're trying to convince and make her less willing to help, let alone listen to your problem. Write a brief word or phrase outline of issues you want to bring up so you don't stray from your main message, which is easy to do when you're upset.

STATE YOUR PROBLEM BRIEFLY AND CLEARLY

After saying you need the person's help, state your problem briefly and clearly. Long explanations will confuse the listener, who may take you less seriously than if you gave a concise explanation of the problem and a reasonable request to address it.

Here is a phone conversation that shows how to negotiate on the phone between Miriam Carter, a parent, and Jayden's fourth-grade teacher, Mr. Stein.

Miriam: I'm hoping you can help me, Mr. Stein. Jayden tells me that two boys in your class are bullying him.

Mr. Stein: Jayden hasn't said anything to me, and I haven't noticed any bullying. Tell him to see me after class tomorrow so we can get to the bottom of it. We'll see who's responsible, and whether it's silly kids' stuff or something more serious.

Miriam: I believe it's serious, but Jayden's afraid to mention it to you. He's small compared to the two kids that pick on him at lunch and recess and ask for test answers in your class. He's thinks they'll harass him more.

Mr. Stein: This sounds like it needs immediate attention, Ms. Carter. I'm glad you called.

Miriam: Thanks. I knew you'd understand, and I appreciate your concern. I'll look forward to hearing from you after you talk to him.

Mr. Stein: I'll also ask the school security guard to observe Jayden and those boys on the playground. After we get the facts, we'll draw up a plan of action with your and Jayden's approval.

Miriam: Thanks. I hope we can solve the problem on this level before it escalates.

Mr. Stein: I believe we can if we work together.

Notice that in this phone dialogue Jayden's mother opens with the words "I'm hoping you can help me." It shows Mr. Stein that she's counting on him to help solve the bullying problem. Miriam also empha-sizes the fact that she considers the problem serious. She lets the teacher know that she appreciates his willingness to find an answer to help her son.

At the close of the conversation, she tells Mr. Stein how she hopes they can solve Jayden's problem with the bullies "on this level," hinting that she'd prefer to address it on the classroom level, and implying that she'll go to the next levels of the school hierarchy, such as the dean of discipline, the assistant principal, or the principal, if she feels the need to escalate her son's case.

BE WILLING TO GO TO THE NEXT LEVEL

After you've exhausted all possibilities, inquire about the chain of com-mand for the organization you're calling. Ask for the name and position of a specific person to whom you should address your problem. If one person isn't responsive, another person will be. More than ever, compa-nies want to please customers. That's why they request feedback by ask-ing you to participate in surveys. They're counting on you to give them positive feedback so that people will see how responsive they are to their customers' needs.

If the person you're speaking to in a phone conversation doesn't help to your satisfaction, ask to speak to a supervisor. In some organizations, the first person you speak to will have some leeway in assisting you, but in others, you'll need to progress up the ladder. For example, in a restau-rant, ask for the manager; in a hospital, ask for the case or nursing super-visor; and in a medical office, ask to speak to the office manager.

It's to a company's advantage to garner positive reviews on online venues because people often base which businesses they'll patronize on the ratings and comments listed on these sites. If you get stuck in nego-tiating for getting what you want, remind the person you're talking to that you plan to write reviews of your experience with their company on Yelp, Angie's List, and other consumer websites, and that you'll inform your friends about how the company responded to your requests. Sometimes, the Better Business Bureau and similar organizations like Angie's List change their rules of operation, so it's wise to research their websites before using them.

Here's an example of a person dissatisfied with a restaurant's food and service and how he dealt with his problem. Keith Walker had a negative experience at a local chain restaurant where he and his friend were dining to celebrate Keith's promotion to sales manager. Keith's chicken Marsala came out overcooked and inedible.

When Keith brought his problem with his dinner to the server's attention, the server offered to bring him another choice within the same price range. However, Keith also found Salisbury steak, the second entrée, not to his liking because it tasted as dry and flavorless as the chicken. When Keith remarked that he'd never had a bad meal at this restaurant and asked what the problem was now, the waiter told him they'd recently acquired a new chef and possibly Keith was used to the previous chef's recipes.

The server said he'd done his best to help him by bringing him another meal and that he didn't see what else he could do to please him. He didn't offer to delete the meal from the check or take the next step of calling his manager. By this time, Keith's patience was wearing thin. Luckily for Keith's friend, his linguini was edible, although the meatballs were as hard as hockey pucks.

Keith didn't have to ask for the manager, Mr. James, because he arrived at the table after he heard the disagreement between Keith and the server. The manager said the food looked fine to him, but that he'd be willing to order a third entrée in the same price range as a one-time courtesy. Keith declined the offer, saying that he didn't want to take a chance on another horrible meal.

The manager grudgingly agreed to remove Keith's entrée from the bill after saying that he was the only customer to complain since he'd worked there. Keith told the manager that he'd heard the restaurant had recently hired a new chef. The manager countered, "That's true, but all of our chefs come highly recommended. They also go through a rigorous training program."

The manager remarked that Keith's friend seemed to enjoy his dinner because he'd noticed that he'd polished off his linguini and sopped up the remaining Bolognese sauce with his roll. Keith's friend told the manager that he didn't see him trying in vain to carve his rock-hard meatball with a steak knife. At least that afforded Keith and friend a chuckle, the high point of their disastrous evening.

By now, Keith's celebratory evening with his friend was ruined. Worse, he wondered if he had any recourse for his bad experience with the restaurant. He figured that escalating his complaint was worth a try to see if he could receive a more equitable compensation. The next day he called the chain restaurant's corporate office to voice his dissatisfaction with his treatment at the restaurant and to request compensation. What follows is a transcript between Keith and Lauren, a guest representative for the Fiesta Americana restaurant chain. He found the phone number of the corporate office by Googling the name of the company.

Keith: Hi, Lauren, I'm Keith Walker from Center City, Philadelphia. I need help with a problem about one of your restaurants, Fiesta Americana, on North Park Street. I'm hoping you can solve my problem so I don't have speak to someone at the next level.

Lauren: I'm here to listen. I'm sorry you had a bad experience, Mr. Walker.

Keith: I'm dissatisfied with the way the waiter and his manager at your Center City restaurant addressed my problem with the dinner I ordered. After receiving two terrible meals, the manager acted like he was doing me a favor when he removed the meal from my bill. He also inspected my friend's platter and remarked that he licked his platter clean, which I thought was inappropriate. I'm smiling now at the absurdity of it, but I'm sure you can understand that it wasn't funny then. My friend couldn't eat the meatballs because they were grossly overcooked like everything else in your restaurant.

Lauren: I understand perfectly, Mr. Walker, and I agree that both the server and manager showed unacceptable behavior. I apologize for how they handled the situation. I can send a gift card that says you can and your friend can order an entrée of your choice, which includes our unlimited Steak and Lobster Feast served with our famous Chocolate Lava Cake for dessert. Would that work?

Keith: That sounds good, Lauren. Thank you very much. However, I hope you understand if I don't hurry back to your restaurant.

Lauren: That's your choice, Mr. Walker, but we hope to regain your trust so that you consider us again soon. I also want you to know that I'll personally talk to the server and the manager and tell them they need to rethink their positions on handling customer complaints. We'll put them in touch with one of our corporate troubleshooters to ensure they know how to treat our patrons fairly.

Keith: How will you know they've taken your suggestions seriously?

Lauren: We'll follow up by monitoring customer feedback and by sending internet surveys to random customers.

Keith: Thanks for your help, Lauren. I enjoyed talking to you despite my experience at the restaurant.

Keith did his best to receive a fair solution from the corporate office since he felt dissatisfied with his treatment at the local chain restaurant. He initiated the conversation by politely asking the representative to help him come to an equitable solution. He set the tone by not overreacting and by stating the problem briefly and concisely. He also addressed the representative by name to personalize the conversation and gain her full cooperation. Most important, he remained calm, rather than accusatory during their discussion.

After talking to Lauren in guest relations, Keith felt satisfied because she listened and agreed to take action by offering him a generous gift card and by speaking to the server and manager about the proper way to address customers' concerns. If Lauren wasn't willing to listen to Keith and understand his dissatisfaction with his dining experience, he would have asked to talk to a higher-up employee in the corporate office. In the end, Keith got what he wanted from the company, an apology and generous compensation for him and his friend.

GET RESULTS WITH MEDICAL PERSONNEL

You can solve your problem with any company if you talk to the right person and remain calm, no matter how upsetting you find your experience. You may also need to go to the next level if you think you're not being treated fairly by a medical practice. People often feel intimidated when they don't feel they're treated fairly in the doctor's office or in the hospital. Sometimes they feel infantilized when a person young enough to be their grandchild calls them by their first name. If that offends you, ask the nurse or doctor to address you with your preferred name. Another problem arises when patients feel that medical personnel don't give them enough information they can readily understand about their medical conditions or take the time to answer questions.

If you aren't satisfied with the quality of care you receive in a medical office, contact the office manager. This person will always be willing to talk to you and help solve your problem.

Picture this: You receive a phone call from your physician's office, but you don't have time to listen to your messages until you get home from the first day of the conference you're attending at 10:00 p.m. on a Friday night. The message the medical technologist left sounds ominous: "Your chest X-ray shows something that concerns the doctor."

The person on the other end of the line (not a doctor, nurse, or physician's assistant, but a medical assistant) says the doctor wants you to have a CAT scan and make an appointment with a pulmonologist. When you look at the scheduled office hours, you learn that the office is closed until Monday at 10:00 a.m. Panic sets in, and you wonder how you'll be able to get through the rest of your conference without suffering anxiety about what the X-ray shows. You need answers, and you need them now.

For the rest of the weekend, you speculate about what could be wrong, and it's always the worst scenario. You indicated on your medical questionnaire from the practice that when you get a message from your doctor you want it to be a detailed one that gives you more information than "The doctor saw something on your X-ray, and you need to have further tests and see a specialist."

On Monday when the office opens, you call, and the receptionist tells you that you have to wait until the medical assistant who called you on Friday arrives, which may not be until the day's end. When you ask for an appointment, the receptionist tells you that the next appointment is in three months. There's no way you're going to wait that long to find out more about your condition and how to remedy it.

When you tell the receptionist you need to talk to the office manager, she immediately connects you. The office manager apologizes for the anxiety you suffered, waiting and wondering why the receptionist left an incomplete message about your X-ray and follow-up. The office manager immediately connects you with your doctor's nurse who reads your chart and tells you that a gray area showed up in your X-ray. He tells you that while the doctor says there's no cause for alarm, you'll need a CAT scan to identify what's causing the abnormality. The nurse also squeezes you in the next day for an appointment when you tell him you can't wait three months.

After speaking to the nurse, you tell the office manager that from now on you'd like to receive messages in accordance with the instructions you listed on your chart when you first signed up with the practice. You want details in the phone message, not bits and pieces that can push your alarm buttons. She tells you she understands and that she'll note it on your chart.

If you have a problem communicating with the office staff, always contact the office manager because that's the main person who can help you resolve problems.

INSTANT REVIEW

Chapter 2: Get Results on the Phone

- Be positive.
- State your problem.
- Be willing to go to the next level.
- Be gracious to the representative.
- Get results with medical personnel.

3

ASK AND RECEIVE FROM A PARTNER

GET YOUR MATE TO OPEN UP

Now that you have techniques for getting what you want in person or on the phone, you're ready to start applying them to different situations you meet on a daily basis.

We'll start with a spouse, partner, mate, or whatever you like to call your significant other. You know your partner better than anyone else does. What in the past has made your partner relate to what you're trying to get across? On the other hand, think of words and phrases you've used that have made your partner flip out, refuse to budge, or ignore you.

How you ask carries equal weight with your words. Don't blame, defame, or intimidate. Back in the day your grandmother may have said this if you tried to get something out of someone: "You can catch more flies with honey than with vinegar." Her advice still holds true, especially when you want something from someone so badly that you may be tempted to throw a tantrum if you don't get it.

Sometimes those old clichés you grew up with guide your life better than current complex psychological theories. Think of sayings you still remember and hand down to your own kids. Regardless of whom you're asking, and especially in the case of a partner, once you let your arguments degenerate into name calling and accusations, the other person will often follow suit in the interest of self-defense.

The more you know a person, the more likely you know that person's sensitive spots and the more you can hurt each other during arguments.

That makes it difficult for you to negotiate and perpetuates hard feelings that linger and may prevent you from gaining success in getting what you want.

You are always in control, and it's up to you to ensure that you both remain civil during a disagreement. It may not seem fair that you have to shoulder the burden of keeping disagreements from snowballing, but it's the best way to ensure that the situation will work out to your advantage. You're the one who's asking, so you need to initiate the change.

Consider this scenario: You believe your partner does not help enough with housework. You're totally exhausted and ready to collapse from working all day. You race home to carpool the kids and pick up the mess everyone left around the house. After all this running around, you know that it's your sole responsibility to figure out what's for dinner (pick up, take out, or make it yourself). Your mate clears the table after dinner, but it's not enough. You've reached your limit, and it's time to act. Think of what Grandmother would do, but make it subtler than giving him an ultimatum to do his fair share around the house or you may meet in divorce court.

Finally, when discussing key issues with your mate, be sure to check in and find out her intention. It can prevent a lot of family discord, particularly between partners. Sometimes, it's easy to assume your partner is thinking one way, when in actuality, she means something entirely different. For example, if your mate questions how much time you're spending with your friends, you might say, "Do you feel I'm not spending enough time with you, or do have another reason for saying that? I just want to understand what you mean."

Sometimes you presume that someone (in this case, a spouse) is criticizing you when she may have a completely different motivation in asking a question. It helps to talk to your spouse and understand exactly what she means when making a statement, rather than presume the worst.

WHEN AND HOW TO ASK

First, catch your partner in a good mood, when he is mellow and relaxed. Figure out the best time to get him to be open to your requests. As in all interactions when you're trying to get someone to agree to your point of view, timing can make a difference in a partner's willingness to agree to your request. While you're eating dinner or before bed is definitely a bad time. First thing in the morning is even worse. Start by saying something like this: "I'd like us to talk about finding a way we can share the housework so I don't feel stressed out and spread thin like I've been feeling lately."

Stop for a minute and wait for his response. Don't pressure, don't cajole; just stop. If your mate agrees to talk, you've scored one; if not, ask when would be a good time, and take it from there. Be sure you set a time right away, or the conversation may never happen. Your partner forgets. Time passes. You forget, and it never comes up again. You want the issue resolved now, or at least you need to settle on a time to discuss it. Ensure that the conversation takes place in a timely manner.

Whenever you decide to talk, be mindfully curious, and ask your partner for suggestions about how he would be willing to help make your life easier. In our house, I'm the chief cook because my spouse prefers cleaning up. He wouldn't know how to chop an onion, roll a meatball, or truss a turkey if his livelihood depended on it. Our arrangement works well for both of us. He also does the laundry because he dirties more clothes than I do. He'd never admit it, but he tosses a towel in the washer after he uses it once.

I buy the groceries because I do the cooking, and he can't tell the difference between iceberg and romaine, and the word *coupon* isn't in his working vocabulary. Think about what's easier for both you and your partner when choosing or renegotiating jobs.

If you don't like the status quo, all jobs are up for grabs. Sometimes you can tire of doing the same job all the time, and you both need a change. Suggest swapping some chores and choosing ones you or your partner would rather do temporarily or permanently.

If it's a case of one of you trying to convince your significant other to take on additional chores so you have more time to go to the gym, play mahjong, or dance around the house in your underwear, ask what chores your partner would be willing to do because as it stands now, you can't keep up the pace and need some relief. At this point, your partner will probably offer to take on an additional household job to placate you because this person is your one and only and wants to please you. The more you're willing to compromise, the more likely your mate will be to meet you halfway.

If your partner doesn't offer to lighten your household load, suggest one or two jobs you think wouldn't require a drastic change in either of your routines. Again, wait for a response. Remember that pausing after you ask is always a good technique because it gives the person you're addressing time to think. It also causes some discomfort. That's helpful too because it appeals to your partner's innate sense of fairness. It may also motivate your one and only to reconsider if he has doubts about compromising or doing things your way.

COMMUNICATE!

Another thing you may want to talk about with your mate is how you're communicating about this and other issues, particularly if things aren't going well between you.

If you usually end up engaging in squabbles about politics, keeping the house neat, or bickering over differences about child-raising techniques, it's time to talk. Usually, but not always, when there's a communication problem, both parties bear some responsibility. Once a vicious cycle of bickering erupts, it's hard to get back to where you were. Of course, if the arguments intensify or happen frequently, you'll want to get professional help.

If communications glitches happen occasionally, sit down with your mate and say what's bothering you. First, ask yourself why you're dissatisfied with the way you're communicating. Is your partner talking more than listening? Does he show anger and ugly moods? Is she aloof and distant? Is she constantly placing blame? Talk about the way you see things, and ask your partner to do the same. Then ask your mate to chronicle his list of grievances calmly and politely as you did yours.

Whatever the problem is, find a good time to broach the subject, and lay out a plan about ways you'd like your communication to improve. Ask your partner to think about what she can do to make things better, and you do the same. Speak calmly and use assertive language, rather than talking harshly or in a mealymouthed way. Avoid blaming your spouse by using the pronoun *I* instead of *you*. (For example, "When you blow up at me for nothing, I feel that you don't care about me," rather than "You're always in a rotten mood because of work and take your anger out on me and the kids.")

Then, just as you do when you want to be sure someone's listening in any important conversation, stop for a moment and let your mate respond. Give your message time to sink in. Sure, sometimes it's awkward and you're itching to jump in and give your opinion, but it's best to wait and give him time to think. If your other half agrees to try harder or at least take what you're saying under consideration, you're on the right track.

If your partner doesn't want to continue talking or doesn't see anything wrong in the way she is acting, ask what it would take for things to get better between you. Now is the time to ask when would be a good time to talk about it because you don't want to continue this way. Press hard on this because you know how important it is. If your spouse doesn't want to set a time, counseling may be the best option to help improve your communication.

DEALING WITH THE KIDS

If you have kids, you know that one partner often takes most of the responsibility for their physical and emotional care. If you're lucky enough to share child-raising responsibilities, count your blessings. However, if you're seeking more help from your partner, you'll want to have that conversation before your children grow up so fast that they won't enjoy the benefits of both parents' love, attention, and wisdom.

If you're the parent who shoulders most of the responsibilities, ask your spouse, no matter how busy, to arrange time with the kids. It can mean something as simple as going out for dessert and asking about what's happening at school and activities. Parent and child can enjoy a shopping trip (to the mall or online) to choose a new outfit or sports equipment. Outings that don't cost money, like going to the library or the park, also prove popular with kids.

Often the parent who's around the kids less time doesn't have the chance to talk about a school subject that's causing a child stress or about an older child's angst about a painful romantic breakup.

Encourage your partner to look for opportunities to spend time alone with each child to create an atmosphere where the child feels comfortable confiding and seeking advice. It can happen en route to a sports event in which they share a mutual interest or after an outing to a restaurant with the parent who's often away from home. Your partner can think of some good possibilities by taking into account mutual interests shared with your child.

Get things moving by providing opportunities for your spouse to bond with the children. That could mean scheduling a family game night with your child or watching a movie that everyone can relate to and enjoy. If your partner's so busy during the week that there's no time for family night, arrange it on a weekend night when everyone's relaxed and doesn't have to worry about their own agendas.

Encourage your partner to listen mindfully when conversing with the kids, to use positive body language, and show good eye contact. Put smartphones away so there are no interruptions. This helps show the kids that both parents care and also sets a positive example in the age of constant texting and social media bombardment that's causing children to have shorter attention spans.

It's also important not to judge or chastise children if you're trying to gain their cooperation. Nobody enjoys being treated harshly or criticized. If you and your spouse want things to run smoothly, listen to your kids when they tell you how they feel about your views. Hear them out even if you don't agree with what they're saying. Of course, you want to let them know what your standards are and reinforce them. If they know you listen to them and truly hear what they say, they'll be more likely to listen to you and comply with your request.

When sharing parenting, if your ideas about the right way to do things differ with those of your spouse, compromise and consider what's best for your child. Spend time building memories no matter how busy you are with your profession and life interests. Your future relationship with your children will thrive because of how they, you, and your partner interact with one other during their formative years.

GET THE INTIMACY YOU CRAVE

Although intimacy is one of the major requirements of an ideal relationship, using the best words to express the need for spiritual and physical intimacy often stymies couples. When faced with a lack of either or both of these ways of expressing closeness, couples drift apart or avoid talking about it, thinking they won't be able solve the problem.

Spiritual intimacy or emotional closeness is the glue that holds your relationship together. Spiritual intimacy doesn't mean you have to agree on everything, such as which TV show to watch, where to go on vacation, or which relatives, his or yours, to visit on your favorite holiday. Rather, spiritual intimacy gives you the feeling that you and your spouse live in sync and enjoy a close connection, much like you felt when you first fell in love, before the bills, job pressures, and the daily pressures you face 24/7. Picture what it would be like to recapture that.

If you want to experience that closeness again, you have to work at it every day, even when you're not in the mood to take time to create a scenario that promotes it. This may mean paying a genuine compliment about something your partner did for you, like cook a gourmet dinner or watch the kids so you can meet up with your friends. Mostly, it means devoting time to each other and feeling like nobody else but the two of you exist in the moment. Enjoying the closeness makes you lose track of time when you're together doing something you both love—something simple, like a walk around the block, or more elaborate, like attending a show or a concert that interests both of you.

As in the case of poor communication, seek therapy if one partner feels unbearably lonely in the relationship due to a lack of spiritual and/or physical intimacy. However, if you believe there's hope, try to get your partner to compromise and give you the attention you want and need. Pick a good time to talk, when your partner's relaxed and not engrossed in another task like watching Monday night football or about to leave for a night out with old friends.

Begin your conversation the way it's helpful to initiate all conversations with a family member or friend when asking for something: Say that something's on your mind and you need to talk about it. Let what your partner says next give you a clue about how to proceed. If your partner reacts negatively or appears disinterested, ask when would be a better time to talk. Make sure to set a time so that the conversation takes place.

If your mate seems open to hearing what you have to say, express your thoughts positively like this, but inject your own words and personality into it: "I feel we're not as close as we used to be, and I'd love to get that feeling back. Do you have any ideas on how we can make it work better for both of us?"

Again, wait for your partner to respond. Whenever you're negotiating with anyone—family member, friend, or service provider—that pause is important. It gives the other person time to digest what you said before responding, and it often cuts into the temptation for either of you to regress into anger.

Be curious. Ask your partner how she feels about bringing more closeness into your relationship. You may want to bring in specific examples of how both of you felt close in the past and what things you can repeat to enjoy those same feelings now and in the future. Maybe you enjoyed watching a favorite TV show together and having a special snack, working in the garden, or going out with friends. Whatever you did that brought you closer, see if it still works. If not, think about building new memories with new experiences.

During your conversation, be sure to use positive body language by adding eye contact and nodding to show you understand your partner's point of view. An important part of mindfulness is putting yourself in another person's place and showing kindness and empathy. When your partner understands that you truly hear what he's saying, he'll be more likely to open up. After your talk, set a time convenient to both of you to meet again to brainstorm new ideas that you both agree to try.

Before you consider rekindling or enhancing your romantic life, it's important to note that without spiritual intimacy it's hard to get into a romantic state of mind. Nothing puts you in the mood for love more than when your brain is wired to connect to your significant other in a deeply emotional way. Who wants to cuddle up with someone who isn't interested in what you're saying and would rather curl up in front of the TV with a bowl of popcorn and watch cable news?

Getting into the right mindset for cuddling, kissing, and its logical progression requires tenderness in the form of loving-kindness and talking to your mate as if there's nobody else in the world but the person with whom you chose to spend your life. It means listening mindfully by giving your full attention to the conversation.

Set a time when you're both relaxed and make room in your life for those times when you can touch, cuddle, and kiss. That's not to say that your romantic session has to take place on the same day every week; that may prove boring and predictable. On the other hand, you may see it as a positive thing because it's something to look forward to. Everybody's different: some partners relish predictability and others delight in surprises. Figure out which type you are and let that knowledge guide you in whether to go by a schedule or approach romance serendipitously.

Think about scheduling emotional and physical closeness as you would anything else, like watching a movie you enjoy, seeing your favorite sports team, or meeting up with friends. The more you connect by scheduling quality time to listen and truly hear one another, the more it will lead to deeper and more satisfying spiritual and physical intimacy.

You've probably figured out that it's not sweet talk and tenderness alone that enhance your physical relationship. You have to set the scene and block out all distractions. That means planning a date night, leaving the kids with Grandmom (or a suitable substitute if Grandmom's busy planning her own date night). It's hard to get in the mood when one of your kids is pounding on your door screaming about a brother who won't stop throwing his pet lizard at her, or another child barging into your room because he saw a black widow spider in his bed. If you want romance, go all out to create the mood.

The bottom line in asking for and getting what you want from your partner in your relationship involves making your best effort to enhance communication by always making yourself open and available. Overlook little faults and foibles in your mate. Everyone has them and needs to look past them to find a partner's best self, the person she fell in love with in the first place. Granted, it isn't always easy, but if you try to keep in mind the qualities that initially drew you to your partner, the easier it will be to rekindle intimacy in your relationship.

It's important to remember when asking and receiving from your mate to be courteous and polite as you need to be in every act of asking with anyone, and to treat your partner as you would a friend. Choose mindfulness principles to help you enjoy the good times and get through the rough spots: active listening with positive body language, assertive speech, nonjudging, patience, putting yourself in the other's place, and, above all, loving-kindness.

INSTANT REVIEW

Chapter 3: Ask and Receive from a Partner

- Find the best way to ask your mate.
- Negotiate household chores.
- Stop for a moment after making your request.

- Give your partner time to think and respond.
- Look for opportunities to share parenting responsibilities.
- Communicate assertively.
- Share parenting duties and reap the joys.
- Practice spiritual intimacy as it's the key to an ideal relationship.
- Schedule time for emotional and physical closeness.
- Use mindfulness principles to help enhance your relationship.

4

GET KIDS TO LISTEN AND DO WHAT YOU WANT

GET YOUR KIDS IN A LISTENING MODE

Dealing with kids isn't always easy, especially when you're trying to get them to do what you want. When you're communicating with kids, or adults for that matter, they're not going to listen until they're ready. You know better than anyone that if they're not listening, you can't get them to do what you want.

You're the one to determine whether your child is in a listening mode, and a few simple steps ensure that. First, be sure she's relaxed and receptive. Say that you want to talk about something important and that you'll be brief. If you ramble on, a kid of any age will tune you out. Plan what you have to say beforehand, and present it using as few words as possible. Kids today live in the electronic age, and their brains aren't wired for long-winded presentations. All effective parents and teachers know the importance of brevity and make their messages sound bites rather than sermons.

Let's go back to the example of the teenage son mentioned in the introduction. He's mouthy, has an answer for everything, and replies in monosyllables. You wonder how you'll get him to study for tests so he doesn't fail. All he wants to do is play video games and hang out with his friends.

Here are a few suggestions: When you talk to a child with the intent of getting him to move in what you consider the right direction, be sure you have your script mapped out so that you present it at his level of understanding. Consider his ability to grasp the importance of what you believe he should do (study for a test, keep his room presentable, or show you greater respect). Impress upon your child of any age that he's the most important person to work on solving the problem you're addressing and that he can and will succeed. Solving the problem on his own with your assistance presents a life lesson for how to address and remediate issues that arise throughout all stages of life.

Speak to your child's level, and give him your best reasons for why you think it's important for him to heed your advice. Above all, be open to listening. Avoid talking too much or talking over him. Often, if teenagers act rebellious or don't want to abide by your requests, it's because they feel they don't have a say in things. Have your teenager give you ideas for solutions and present your own, a win-win situation.

SET THE STAGE FOR COOPERATION

Things don't happen in a vacuum, and it's the same with getting kids to cooperate without them staging a ruckus that rattles your nerves and your eardrums. Setting the stage for gaining your child's cooperation is important if you want to get her on your side. No matter how she tries your patience, treat her politely, speak calmly, and expect the same from her.

When your child cooperates and shows you her best self, praise her efforts and tell her how much you appreciate her willingness to meet you halfway. Catch her doing something good, like clearing the table without your having to remind her or showing a friend or family member kindness by offering to help someone in need.

Acknowledging your child's positive behaviors will give him a strong incentive for showing willingness to comply with your requests. It will also give you leverage when it's time to gain your child's cooperation for issues that may prove more of a challenge, such as getting him to pay more attention to his homework so he earns better grades or spending more time with the family instead of hiding out in his room texting or playing video games with friends.

SAY WHAT YOU MEAN AND STAND BY IT

If you mention a consequence (called a punishment back in the day) for your child's not going along with your ideas, be sure it's realistic and one that you'll carry out. Always say what you mean and stand by it. To do otherwise hurts your credibility, especially with kids, as they're quick to see through you.

Above all, don't say tell a child that if she does something you don't approve of, you'll confiscate her phone for a year if you have no intention of doing so. Think of a reasonable, yet meaningful, consequence that doesn't last into perpetuity, and mete it out fairly. Better yet, ask your child what he would do in your situation if the roles were reversed. Sometimes kids can come up with creative ideas that work.

PLAN YOUR STRATEGY IN ADVANCE

In chapter 1 we discussed the importance of using key words and phrases to get people on your side so they'll cooperate. Follow these steps to get your child to see things your way:

- Think through your plan carefully before presenting it.
- Choose your words carefully. You know your child and how best to appeal to him. What has worked in the past? What hasn't worked? What do you think will work now?
- Find a time when your child's relaxed and receptive.
- Start out by using key words and phrases. Say, "I want to talk to you about something important," or "I'd like to talk about something that concerns both of us." Mainly, stay calm. When you're dealing with kids, especially older ones, avoid pulling rank and giving ultimatums. It never works.
- Tell your child what you want her to do as briefly as possible. Be assertive, not passive, and not pushy.
- Listen to what your child has to say. Don't argue or put yourself on his level. Be the grown-up.
- If your child backtracks, revisit the issue, always with patience and politeness even if she pushes your buttons.

HOW PARENTS DEALT WITH A CHILD'S FAILING NOTICE

Here is a conversation between Ava, Shawn, and their son Chandler, age thirteen. See how these parents handled their son's homework problem.

Chandler races to his room past his parents who wait for him to come home from the bus stop.

Shawn: Stop right there, buddy. Mom and I need to talk to you. Have a seat.

Chandler grudgingly flops onto the living room sofa.

Chandler (frowning): What did I do this time? According to you two, I never do anything right.

Ava (taking a seat next to him): We found this in the mail today.

She passes a letter from his middle school principal to her son.

Shawn: It looks like you're failing two subjects, Spanish and math, if you don't do something to improve your grades now.

Chandler (crumbling up the paper and tossing it on the floor): I hate school. It's boring, and those teachers are mean. I hate equations. When will I ever use them? Spanish is not my thing. You have to memorize all these vocabulary words nobody ever heard of and pass impossible tests every week.

Ava: I know you're no fan of school this year, but we want to help you in any way we can. We need to talk about this now or tonight after dinner. You pick the time. We can solve the problem together.

Chandler: Let's do it now. I want to get it over with. You two are always bugging me about something.

Shawn: We'll make it quick and painless. We'll say what we have to say and hope you consider it. All we ask is that you listen and help yourself figure out a way to pass math and Spanish.

Chandler: Are you going to take away my phone and video games? That's the first thing you do if I'm not the perfect child and do things your way. You don't think I do anything right. My friends' parents don't bug their kids like you do. You're always on my back.

Ava: I'm sure your friends' parents are concerned about their kids like we are about you. And yes, you *do* do a lot of things right. For one thing, you take care of the dog and take out the trash. You're also a great baseball player or you wouldn't have made the JV team.

Chandler stifles a smile.

Shawn (putting his hand on his son's arm): And no, we're not going to take away your electronic gadgets this time. This calls for stronger measures. We're going to do whatever we can to help you so you pass all your subjects, but you'll have to do most of the work.

Ava: We also believe that nobody's perfect, and we don't expect you to be perfect, as you put it. We all have room to improve. We're not asking you to do anything impossible. That's why we want to get your ideas about what you can do to pass math and Spanish.

Chandler retrieves the failing notice from the floor and smooths it out. He puts it on the coffee table.

Shawn (waiting a moment for Chandler to read the paper from the principal): For starters, we'll contact both teachers of the classes you're failing and get them to recommend tutors who can help you pass your tests.

Ava: We'll also ask both your teachers to put you on a daily report to tell us how you're doing in their classes each day. They'll give you a letter grade for each day's work and write a brief comment about how you did in class that day. If they see a problem, we can catch it before it gets worse.

Shawn: Now we're coming to the most important part of the puzzle. Son, what can *you* do to help yourself pass these subjects?

Chandler: Can I think about it awhile?

Ava: It's too late for that. We need you to tell us now.

Shawn: We have to start working on our plan today. We're all in this together, but you're the most important player in this story.

Chandler (taking a few moments to think): For one thing, I can pay more attention in class and do my homework even though I don't like those subjects.

Ava: Anything else?

Chandler: I could talk to both of my teachers about some makeup work and stay after school with them once in a while to get extra help.

Shawn: It would also help if you told them you're going to try hard to pass and you know you can if you put your mind to it.

Chandler (rolling his eyes): That too, Dad. I'll sound like a real kiss-up, but I guess if I want to pass, I have to do some things I don't like.

Ava: It's not for that reason you're doing it, son. It's to let your teachers know you're ready to give it your best effort.

Chandler: Okay. I hear you, but I'm not going to like doing it.

Shawn: If we can help in any way, let us know. We want you to pass, but you have to want it more.

Chandler: I don't like the thought of summer school more than I dislike those subjects, so I'm going to do my best.

Ava: That's good enough for us—and for you.

Chandler (racing up the stairs and turning midway to look at his parents): Thanks.

Ava and Shawn smile at one another and move to the kitchen to make dinner.

Shawn and Ava made Chandler a partner in solving his problem of how to strive toward better grades in math and Spanish. They built him up rather than diminishing or berating him. They came up with solutions, such as talking to his teachers and going to tutoring, but he had to agree to do most of the work.

His parents complimented him on his strong points and demonstrated their confidence in him while insisting that he take on the major responsibility of passing his subjects. They viewed the problematic event of a possible school failure in the larger context of a life lesson about self-confidence and perseverance that he would carry with him for the rest of his life.

TRY THIS IF NOTHING ELSE WORKS

When a child constantly acts out or doesn't cooperate, try backing off until he comes around. Try this only if lack of cooperation and defiance is a chronic, severe, ongoing problem. Don't be overly solicitous or attentive. Most kids crave attention, and if you give them too much positive or negative attention, your plan to help them cooperate may backfire.

Praise your child when she cooperates, but act neutral and don't be overly effusive. Observe how she reacts when she doesn't get your attention by showing negative behavior. Seek professional help if you feel that the problem with your child proves too difficult to handle on your own.

Also, remember to choose your conflicts. Calling your kids out for trivial things will not help your cause of getting them to embrace your ideas. Give them some leeway in making their own decisions, but make sure you're with them to guide them along the way, as the parents in the previous anecdote were when they helped their son resolve his problem with failing grades. If you give them a reasonable degree of freedom in deciding what's best for themselves, they'll often surprise you. Of course, if they consistently make bad decisions or ones you think would harm them, you'll need to intervene.

Sometimes kids don't want to listen, and when they get in that mode, there's not much you can do until they come to their senses or grow up a little. With good planning and using a few simple techniques like the ones mentioned, you can get your kids to cooperate, but if things move too slowly or you're not satisfied with the outcome of your efforts, try doing something outrageous.

My high school teaching experience taught me how being outrageous can help you deal with kids when conventional methods don't work. Maybe your child has a strong will and won't cooperate, has inherited the stubborn gene, or likes doing things his own way with no interference.

Ben Marshall, my department head at school, had a student office aid, Liam, who acted boisterous and silly when he got in one of his zany moods. Teachers trying to get their paperwork done in the English department office during their free periods got annoyed by Liam's antics and complained about his behavior to our leader. Ben, my boss, thought of the brilliant idea to feed into his helper's silliness to gain his attention and hopefully help him calm down.

One day when Liam started joking around with Mr. Mortimer, one of the more stern, strict members of our department, my boss ran out from behind his desk, played a rock-and-roll song from his oldies music collection, and danced Liam around the room. That unexpected, spontaneous action shocked Liam into changing his behavior, at least for the time being. It had a long-term effect on him since it helped him realize how his actions affected the people who came into the office expecting a work-conducive environment. Mr. Mortimer cracked a smile for the first time since I've known him at the absurd but effective method Ben used as a teachable moment for Liam.

How can you as a parent use outrageous behavior to your advantage? Maybe you've heard how some ingenious parents of toddlers and younger kids used unconventional behavior to get their kids to stop throwing tantrums in public or private. These inventive parents simply imitated their children's embarrassing antics by hurling themselves on the ground, shaking their fists, and screaming until their kids came to their senses.

Try it if you have youngsters who try your patience at home or at the grocery store, but be prepared for fallout from less brave family members and parents who witness your tirade. Do whatever works—in this case, acting outrageous—and more power to you for being brave enough to try.

You can try a tamer version of imitating a child's tantrum by standing over the child if she's lying on the ground or staring her down if she's standing. All you have to do is shout louder and drown her out. Eventually, she'll probably relent out of desperation and embarrassment if other people witness her outburst—and yours.

Of course, it's much easier to act outrageous with little ones. Older kids may miss the point completely and laugh in your face if you embarrass yourself trying to get them to come around to your point of view. Is there anything you can do that's out of the ordinary that will help bigger kids get the message? You can shoot back at them when they respond with nasty words, such as "I hate you, you [fill in the blank with your teen's favorite epithet]."

Try saying, "I love you, but I won't put up with how you're acting. When you're ready to talk, let me know, and I'll listen and give you the same courtesy I expect from you." My mom said this to me when I tried her patience by asking for impossible privileges, like attending a drive-in movie (Mom called it the passion pit) with a hot guy when I was a teenager, or going to a party where they played kissing games like spin the bottle and post office in my friend's basement where parents were nowhere in sight. It worked for my mom, who never lost an argument, and it can work for you if your teenager's receptive to a good old-fashioned guilt trip.

Here's another thing you can do with both little kids and older ones when they lose control: let out big belly laughs until they start laughing themselves. It worked for my neighbor when her child threw a tantrum in a dollar store about not getting a toy she wanted, and it can work for you. Dream up some outrageous responses to use with your own kids when nothing else gets their attention.

Getting your kids to do what you want can be daunting, but if you plan ahead, catch them at the right moment, and use mindfulness principles such as patience, assertive talk, and loving-kindness, you're on your way to reaching them and gaining their cooperation.

INSTANT REVIEW

Chapter 4: Get Kids to Listen and Do What You Want

- Prepare your kids to listen.
- Stay positive to promote cooperation.
- Stand by what you say, and don't give in.
- Try stepping back.
- Cut your kids some slack.
- Encourage them to make their own good decisions.
- If all else fails, act outrageous.

5

NEGOTIATE PRICES AND SERVICE CONTRACTS

REVIEW THE BASICS OF ASKING

If you don't want to pay top dollar for services and contracts, you can use your negotiating skills to deal with prices on anything from cars to vacation condo rentals. Additionally, it's important not to leave your cable, internet, and phone bills to chance. Check them over when they come due, and prepare to do some serious negotiating with your providers. You may be taken aback when the cost of your bill rises astronomically because you didn't anticipate the precipitous rise in price. With your new skills that help you ask and get what you want, you'll come out a winner.

Now that you're familiar with techniques for negotiating in person and on the phone, you know effective ways to get service providers of all types to listen and grant you what you want. The most important qualities that will make the person you're asking more receptive to giving you what you want are: always show your best side by being calm and polite; make your case briefly and succinctly; speak assertively; and use "magic words" such as " I hope you can help me," or "I need to talk with you about . . ." You'll also enjoy inventing your own magic words that complement your personality. When talking in person to those providing goods and services, remember to build rapport with eye contact and positive body language.

As demonstrated in previous chapters, you can be equally effective on the phone by using curiosity, a mindfulness trait. As you talk with the representative on the phone, you can often tell something about his personality by his words, responses, and tone of voice. Let your common sense and intuition guide you in how to proceed with your pitch as he reveals himself to you in conversation. Also, be aware of his language patterns, how he speaks, and the types of words he uses. Try to use the same type of wording and sentence structure since people gravitate more to those who act as they do, whether they're politicians or service providers. Similarly, if you need to correspond in writing via letter, email, or text to service providers, try to mimic their wording and writing style.

NEGOTIATE HOME SERVICES

If you own a home, unless you prefer to do things yourself, you'll need special services periodically, such as lawn workers or snow removal people. Always talk about the price before the person starts the job and see what discounts you can get. If you consider the price too high, tell the company that you'd like to hire them because you've heard good things from neighbors about their work but that the price is too high. Ask the representative what she can do to make the cost more affordable.

Say something along these lines: "I like the lawn cutting/snow removal that you do in my neighborhood, but the price is too high for my budget. What can you do to help me hire you by making it more reasonable?" Always make your request brief and to the point. Talking too much or in a passive manner will make you sound weak and ineffective.

Pause to give the person a chance to respond. Don't talk or worry that you're making the representative uncomfortable. She wants your business and would likely prefer providing services at a reduced rate rather than lose the job. After you've struck a deal you're comfortable with, thank the person and ask for a business card to give to your friends.

ASK FOR A BETTER PRICE FOR PRODUCTS YOU WANT

When you go to a restaurant, search for a coupon in the newspaper or the internet first. Be sure to ask your server if the company has an app that offers benefits for frequent diners. Once you give a restaurant your email address, they'll send you coupons on a regular basis and for special occasions, like your birthday and anniversary. Also, some restaurants offer punch cards or dining clubs that offer a free entrée if you patronize the establishment regularly.

Before you order, ask if there are any promotions going on. A popular chain restaurant recently offered a burger and fries for five dollars while a smaller children's lunch costs much more than that. Sometimes hunger pangs get the best of you, and you don't notice any flyer specials on the table placed right in front of you, so it helps to ask.

You can also negotiate a better price with furniture and bedding companies. These companies offer excellent opportunities to bargain in good faith. Before committing to what you consider an exorbitant sticker price, ask the salesperson what discounts are available on the day you shop. Explore store, holiday, or senior citizen discounts, for example. Some companies will match their competitors' prices. Prepare ahead of time by perusing the print, TV, and internet ads.

Yard sales and thrift shops are often willing to reduce prices to make a sale and are open to bargaining. Ask for what you consider a fair price, but be reasonable. People want to make a profit, but they don't want to give the item away. Say, "Would you accept five dollars for these jeans? I'd love to buy them as they fit perfectly, but I'm not [able/willing] to spend double that price. Can you help me lower the price?" It never hurts to ask. If the person isn't willing to discount the item further, ask what she thinks a fair price would be; then, either pay it or walk away. It's your choice.

Are you looking for a car to buy or rent? Before you commit yourself to high payments, research car costs on a reputable website and compare prices in different dealerships. Gather all the information you can from reputable organizations that know the business, such as Edmunds, Kelley Blue Book, Motor Trend, CarsDirect, and Consumer Reports, which you can find online. Also, check online for lists of government recalls to see which vehicles had recent problems so that you can avoid them.

Armed with the information you collect, go to the car dealership prepared to discuss trade-in rates, car price, and warranty rates. Ask the dealer what extras and perks they're prepared to give you to close the deal, in addition to the best price possible. Offer 3 to 5 percent (3 percent is the overall average) above the dealer's true car cost. It's not a big profit, but many dealers will agree to it. Don't calculate your offer from the factory invoice because that is not the price the dealer paid. The invoice price of the car isn't the dealer's actual true cost. Edmunds, an online resource for information about cars, will help you figure out the true cost. See this online site: https://autocheatsheet.com/new-car/factory-invoice.html#dealer-cost-4.

A hot-selling car may have little room for negotiation, while you may be able to go even lower with one that isn't flying off the car dealer's lot.

If you've done all you can and you're not satisfied with the dealer's final offer, walk away. Sometimes the salesperson will ask you to come back. You've made a good decision either way.

When negotiating prices for vacation homes and condos, you may be tempted to turn to online sites, such as Vrbo (for rent by owner) and Airbnb. Be sure to check to see if the rental sites you consult carry a booking fee to the organization sponsoring the rentals. If you dislike the thought of paying a fee, research some nonfee organizations online: Google "non-fee-charging vacation rentals."

If you decide to book your vacation rental through a real estate agent or owner, there's a lot of room for discussion about the cost of your rental. Ask the owner or real estate agent if she can give you a discount for a longer stay. Tell her how much you like the property but will need them to lower the price if they want you to consider it. Be sure to ask about last-minute rentals and cancellations. Often, you can get them for a much lower rate.

Some condo fees are nonnegotiable, but you can try asking for better terms of payment and/or a later departure date. The next time you look for a vacation rental, negotiate with the real estate agent or owner using the techniques in this book. You'll be surprised how many benefits and perks you can discuss and win by skillful bargaining techniques.

Now, we'll move on to your cable company, which often proves the most challenging business to hammer out a settlement with. Cable companies will often surprise you with an increase in your bill every year when your contract's up for renewal. Don't panic because once you negotiate your deal, you can ask them to reimburse you for the up-front money you paid for the new contract. If you subscribe to a cable provider for your TV, internet, and possibly phone, aim to make the best agreement possible with or without a contract.

Take the first step and compare prices the cable competitors offer. Look online or call the companies to learn their terms and exactly what you get from them. Arm yourself with all the statistics, and be ready to quote them to your own company when trying to get the best price and benefits.

Begin your negotiating by calling the 800 customer service department, and say you're calling to renew your current contract with the cable company but as it stands, the price is much too high. Use all the techniques you've learned in this book by acting polite and professional. Say you'd like to remain a customer as you've been a loyal one for many years and that you'd rather stay with them than change to a new company.

Tell the representative exactly what you're looking for in your ideal package. Be willing to compromise on certain services if they cost appreciably more than you want to pay. However, be sure to ask for extra perks, such as a free DVR or channels you have that you can't live without. Also, ask the representative to throw in one or more free channels for a limited time period so you can try them. Inquire about bundles (packaging of different services) and see which one works best for you. You may not need your landline and opt for double play (TV and internet) rather than being stuck with an extra phone you rarely use.

If you don't get satisfaction from the 800 number, call back and say, "Cancel service" to the person or robot answering the phone. They'll quickly put you in touch with someone who is willing to listen because the company doesn't want to lose your business. Repeat your request to the "Cancel Service" department, telling the representative you're willing to switch to one of their competitors if they aren't willing to compromise and give you a fair price on your package. In most cases, they will do their best to accommodate you.

If you don't get any satisfaction talking to the retention/loyalty department (or whatever your company calls the office that attempts to keep customers happy) or the "Cancel Service" line, contact the Office of the President (find the number online) and talk to the representative about getting the same rate you've been paying or an even lower rate.

Ask him to tell you about the best package that's currently available. Explain all the things you're looking for in a package while keeping the price reasonable. This will be your final resort if you haven't reached an agreement with the other departments you've contacted. Then it's your decision whether to stay with the company or move to another company more receptive to your requests.

Here's a conversation between customer Tara Silver and Ryan, a rep at the 800 level, to show you how Tara navigates the system to attempt to get what she wants from the company and persists until she gets it:

Tara: Hi, my name is Tara Silver, and I want to lower my cable package. I've been with you for ten years and would like to stay because I enjoy your great selection of free movies. However, I'm looking at your competitor's prices and see that if I signed up with them, I could get the same channels you're giving me for fifty dollars less.

Ryan: First, I'd like to thank you for being a loyal customer all these years. I'm willing to hear what you have to say, but first, I want to point out that the internet speed you're getting with us is much higher than our major competitor's. Let me ask you a question, Ms. Silver, Do you use the internet for work, and are you happy with our great speed?

Tara: I like it, but I'm willing to go with a slightly lower speed if you could give me a better price than what I'm currently paying. Two hundred a month is beyond my budget, and I need you to reduce my bill.

Ryan: I hear you, Ms. Silver, but at this time, we have no other plans available at a lower price. Call back in a couple of months and we'll let you know what we have to offer. If you'd consider giving up some of your premium channels, I may be able to do something you'd find acceptable right now.

Tara: I'm not doing that. I'd rather go with a company that's more receptive to customers.

Tara isn't giving up. She makes a second call by telling the robot on the phone to cancel service. Almost immediately, Jaimie, a representative from the retention department, greets her in a pleasant voice.

Jaimie: I see you made a call to our cancellation division. Before you do that, I'd like to see what we can do to help you change your mind.

Tara: I'll do that only if you'll give me a better rate for my bundled cable package.

Jaimie: Unfortunately, as I can see that Ryan told you from my notes, your current package is the best one we have at this time. How about if I throw in six months of Netflix? You can cancel it when the free offer is over, or you can opt to pay the small fee of ten dollars a month for it.

Tara: I don't consider a hundred and twenty dollars a year extra for an additional channel a great bargain. I'll pass on that. Ryan told me that I can call back at a later date to see if you have more reasonable packages. Can you do that for me now as a courtesy as I've been with you a long time?

Jaimie: I apologize, Ms. Silver, but as Ryan said, what you're paying is the best offer we have at this time. I hope you'll reconsider. I'm sure we can get you a better deal in a couple of months if you can hang on.

Tara: I appreciate your willingness to help me, but this isn't working. I'm going to think about it. Thanks for your help.

Jaimie: Thanks for being a loyal customer. I hope you don't leave us.

Tara: It may come to that.

Tara isn't about to give up on her mission to lower her cable bill. She believes that in all attempts at negotiation, you should start at the first level and work your way up to the top. She finds the phone number to the Office of the President online and calls. A young man named Jamal answers.

Tara: I'm hoping you can help me, Jamal. Please call me Tara. I've talked to some people in your company and as a longtime customer, I'm not satisfied with the level of help I've received. In fact, the retention department's offer wasn't much better than the 800 number's offer.

Jamal: I hear you, and I understand your frustration. You've come to the right place, Ms. Tara. Tell me the problem, and I'll see what I can do to help you.

Tara: Thank you, Jamal. I appreciate your willingness to help me. I need you to help me get my cable bill down to what it was or lower than before I got the astronomical bill that just came in the mail.

Jamal: Excuse me for a moment while I look over the services you had before the rate increase.

Tara: Take all the time you need. I want to come to an agreement today or, as I told the last rep, I'll cancel and switch to your main competitor.

Jamal: We don't want you to leave us. I'll do everything I can to keep you as a customer. Before I look at your previous package, I'd like you to tell me what you most want to keep and wouldn't be willing to drop in your services.

Tara: I want a couple of premium channels like the ones I have now, a sports channel, and the main cable news channels. I also want to keep the free movies, especially the old classics.

Jamal (looking over her previous bills): Would you be willing to go with one premium channel and go with the double instead of the triple play that includes your phone?

Tara: I'd agree to that. How much would that reduce my bill?

Jamal: We can reduce it by twenty dollars a month, but you'd still get all the other benefits you had under the old contract.

Tara: Can you throw in Netflix?

Jamal: I can give it to you free for one year. I can also take the DVR fee off your bill for the six months. How does that sound?

Tara: You have a deal, Jamal. I'll miss my other premium channel, but I certainly won't miss the landline phone with all the nuisance calls I get. Will you be willing to reimburse me for the extra I paid this month? That bill was a shocker.

Jamal: No problem, Ms. Tara. It will take a couple of billing cycles, but I'll put in the paperwork today for your refund. I'll also add a twenty-dollar credit to your first bill for staying with us. We value your business.

Tara: Thanks for all your help today, Jamal. I enjoyed talking with you.

Jamal: You're very welcome. Remember to call us a month in advance of when your one-year contract expires so you don't find any surprises in your bill next year.

Tara: I'll write a note on my calendar. Thanks again, Jamal.

Tara found a successful resolution to her problem with the cable company by showing patience, being pleasant, and making her case briefly and succinctly. She started her quest for a more reasonable bill at the lower levels of the cable company, and when she wasn't satisfied with the answers at the 800 and retention levels, she called the corporate office, where she finally came to an agreement with Jamal.

In addition to your cable bill, you may also want to consider negotiating your cell phone bill. Use the same procedure you did for coming to an agreement on your cable bill. If one division doesn't help, another usually will. If you don't know whom to call next, ask the previous representative. Tell the person you're not satisfied with her answer and would like to speak to the supervisor or the next level.

Usually, you'll find the phone company as willing to compromise as the cable company did. Be sure to ask for any discounts they have, such as AARP, AAA, or ones for teachers, veterans, or senior citizens. Speak mindfully as Tara did with the cable company representatives. Also, do your homework, and be well prepared with statistics from other wireless companies you've talked to on the phone or at their kiosks at the mall. Take the literature home that they give you, and highlight the key points so you have the facts and figures before you when you consult your cell phone company.

You can negotiate anything, even what seems like fixed prices in department stores, with or without a coupon. It requires time, patience, and perseverance like what Tara accomplished in her dealings with the cable company. Once you get used to negotiating and reaping the benefits, you'll become a pro and want to negotiate all your services. Moreover, you'll begin to enjoy asking for and receiving what you want.

INSTANT REVIEW

Chapter 5: Negotiate Prices and Service Contracts

- Review the basics of asking before you negotiate.
- Negotiate home services.
- Get good offers from restaurants.
- Find better deals at yard sales and thrift shops.
- Save money on your next car.
- Find the best price on vacation rentals.
- Save money on your cable and phone bills.

6

CONTACT A COMPANY
ABOUT A CONCERN

COMPLIMENT OR COMPLAIN ABOUT A COMPANY

When I taught high school, my most popular lesson involved writing letters of compliment or complaint to companies about their products. After students sent letters to local and national companies, the businesses rewarded them with pleasant surprises, such as cases of soft drinks, cookies, and coupons for foods they loved. One grateful student received an autographed book by a popular auto racer.

Class members found it interesting that whether students gave the company compliments or complaints, they were both rewarded, although those who had positive things to say received more gifts they considered valuable. Students wrote letters to help them hone their writing skills, which they agreed were probably more effective than texts or emails. Handwritten letters draw more attention and responses to your concerns than communicating with companies by text or email.

If you believe that a product is superior or inferior and wish to contact the company to let them know, write them a letter explaining your main points of satisfaction or dissatisfaction and your experiences using the product. You'll probably hear from them because their main goal is pleasing their customers. You may be lucky enough, as my students were, to receive free samples, whether you write to give them a compliment or complaint. For you, calling them is better than sending an email or text as it will be easier to contact them since they receive many emails and texts, which makes it difficult to get back to you in a timely manner.

Remember to practice mindfulness whichever way you prefer to communicate. Write or speak assertively rather than aggressively or passively, and choose your words carefully. State your opinions briefly and courteously, and remind the customer service worker that you'll look forward to hearing from them soon. Request samples whether you're praising the company or expressing dissatisfaction with their product. Ask for a refund in cash or coupons if the product didn't work for you.

FIX AN INFERIOR FOOD PRODUCT PROBLEM

What can you do to get satisfaction if a food product is not to your liking? Recently, my neighbor Shawn purchased a box of powdered mashed potatoes to accompany the prepared turkey breast he bought at the supermarket. He followed the directions to a T but discovered to his dismay that the potatoes turned out watery and inedible. Of course, he poured the mushy mess down his garbage disposal. Shawn invited his friend for dinner and told him that he'd planned to make homemade mashed potatoes but didn't have time, so a box of "fluffy, buttery mashed potatoes" enticed him at the store.

He'd never bought powdered potatoes before, but since he was pressed for time, he thought he'd try them. As he opened a can of candied yams to accompany the turkey, his friend suggested calling the company, one that also makes popular cake and muffin mixes, and telling them what happened. His friend had called a similar company and found the customer service division willing to reimburse him for the product that didn't turn out to his liking.

The next day Shawn took his friend's advice and called the company; they rewarded him with a few generous coupons for his inconvenience. The rep apologized and said that it was rare for their potatoes to turn out watery. Keith didn't want to take a chance on buying another box of potatoes, so he asked the rep to send him coupons for their cake and frosting mixes, which he often used.

Along similar lines, I once purchased a frozen stuffed shrimp dinner that contained cocktail sauce. When I opened the container, the sauce was a bilious yellow color. The company fully reimbursed me for the product and sent extra coupons for more seafood dinners.

Sometimes you buy a product, like cosmetics at the drugstore, and the color looks ghastly on you. You've already opened the product and think you can't return it. However, many drugstores have a policy stating that you can return cosmetics, even opened ones if they aren't right for you.

If you're dissatisfied with any food product, call the customer service number on the package or find it on the internet. You'll get satisfaction every time if you use magic words and state your case briefly and assertively.

RESOLVE YOUR ISSUES AT THE AUTO BODY SHOP

Have you ever bought a car that wouldn't qualify for the lemon law but caused you problems that inconvenienced you to the point of total frustration? For example, you replaced a tire and had to return to the shop many times to eliminate the light that kept appearing on your dashboard, indicating that the tire lacked enough air, when the tire was filled to capacity.

If annoying problems like these surface with your car, ask for the manager. Consult the same manager on all your visits to the shop, and establish good rapport with this key person. My friend Lauren found it helpful to befriend the manager when she encountered problems after taking her car to the quick-care center for routine inspections at the dealership, or for minor matters, such as tire rotation.

In the past, Lauren found the quick-care center that was connected but independent of the main repair shop incompetent at doing routine inspections and making the repairs she requested. She asked the receptionist to see the manager. After the receptionist took her to the main desk and introduced her to Drew, the manager, he immediately started a case for her. He gave her personalized attention beyond what she anticipated she'd receive from the busy car company. From then on, Lauren always contacted Drew when she had a problem. He always did his best to help her by asking Rocky, his lead mechanic, to handle her case.

If you're not satisfied with service at a garage, always consult the manager, who should give you personalized care and ensure that you're taken care of every time. Be sure to give the manager credit due by filling out a glowing evaluation for him and specifically mentioning what he did to help you.

REDO A BAD HAIR DAY

Have you ever returned from the beauty shop or barbershop with an unflattering cut, dye job, or both? If you're like I am, you feel like staying in the house until it grows out and you look like yourself again, rather than a character from an *Addams Family* rerun (à la Morticia or Cousin Itt). When you look in the mirror and feel like screaming, "Is that really me?" it's time to take action.

My friend Isabella did just that. She needed her hair cut and dyed because she was up for a promotion for a management position and wanted to look her best, but her hairdresser Jo wasn't working that day. The personnel director had scheduled an impromptu interview the next day with her prospective employer. She asked for the usual, a short, curly bob with long layers with a subtle ash brown color, highlighted with blonde. When Martha, the stylist, finished and showed her her new style and color, Isabella said loudly to all within earshot, "Yikes! What have you done?"

Isabella had no inkling when Martha applied the color that it was black instead of ash brown because the dye in the container looked the same as it always did, a neutral off-white. Martha had spun Isabella around in the swivel chair and turned her away from the mirror so she couldn't see her new cut and color until she'd completed it. The stylist hoped that her client would react with gleeful surprise when Martha showed her how she looked in the mirror. Martha expressed shock at her client's reaction. What was wrong with Isabella? Didn't she appreciate a quality stylist when she saw one?

The curly bob Isabella requested turned out to look more like a super-short pixie that made her prominent features appear stark and gave her a severe look that didn't match her warm personality and reputation of an employee who looked like someone accessible and approachable, someone an employer would gladly hire.

Listen to the conversation at the beauty shop:

Martha (frowning): You don't like it?

Isabella: It certainly isn't what I expected. If I'd known you were going to do this, I wouldn't have let you touch my hair. I don't know what my prospective employer will think of me when I go on my interview. I look like a grumpy schoolmarm.

Martha: You have to be kidding, hon. I've been in this business since before you were born. You can see how many loyal customers I have. I thought you'd like having a fresh new image. Darker hair is fashionable and sophisticated. Highlights can age you. As for the short bob you wanted, don't you think it's a little old fashioned? Nobody asks for it nowadays. It looks like a flapper from the twenties.

Isabella: I told you exactly what I wanted, and now I'll have to go to my interview wearing a scarf or a turban.

Martha: I thought you'd be pleased with a look that I thought suited you better. When you said you had an interview coming up, I figured that a stylish, updated look would help get you the job. I didn't mean to make you unhappy.

Isabella: Truthfully, I'm very disappointed. I don't think I should have to pay for this hairstyle that may hinder my attempt to get a promotion.

Martha: If you have so little confidence that you think you won't get the job because of a new hairstyle, I feel sorry for you.

Isabella: I'd like my money back, all seventy dollars of it. Then I'd like to speak to the manager to see if she can undo the damage you did.

Martha: Sorry, the manager's off today, but you can talk to Rona, our senior stylist and assistant manager, to see what she can do to refund your money and change your style. Remember, hon, hair grows quickly. It won't stay this way forever.

Martha confers with Rona, the senior stylist, and brings her over to talk with Isabella, who again expresses her dissatisfaction with the cut and color.

Rona: Martha told me you want your money back. I'm sorry for the inconvenience. I think it looks great, but if you don't like it, I'm willing to refund your money. I'm sure the manager would agree. However, your hair is very dark now, and it would require a lot of work to lighten it. Highlights may damage your hair after I lighten it. We can go down a shade or two, but it won't look exactly the way you pictured it would.

Isabella: I'm very upset about this and will think twice before returning to your shop even though I'm satisfied with Jo, my regular stylist. What can you do about the style? I've never been a pixie kind of person. The twenties look is more my style.

Rona (running her hands through Isabella's hair): There's still a little length there. We can trim it with a few layers and scrunch it to give it some curl and body. It won't be what you're used to, but I'll do the best I can.

Isabella: Thanks. I'm willing to try.

Martha: I'm truly sorry for the inconvenience. I hope you'll come back to your regular stylist.

Isabella: Thank you. No offense, but I hope you'll think twice before giving someone the new look that you like and consider what they like instead.

Martha: I hear you, although many of my customers enjoy being adventurous and like going for a new look.

Isabella: That may be true, but I know what I like and expect to get it when I'm paying this much for a cut and color. Thanks, Rona. Let's get this job done. I can't wait to see how it turns out.

Rona: It may take a while, but I'm going to do my best to keep you coming to our salon.

In this encounter at the hair salon, Isabella expressed her strong disappointment about the services Martha rendered. She told her in an assertive manner that she wanted her money back and wanted a redo of the style and color. Isabella left the salon with a more acceptable color (medium ash brown) and a spiffy short, curly cut that would be easy to maintain with a user-friendly gel and scrunch regimen. In fact, she liked the cut and color so much that she told Rona she'd consider getting it again.

REMEDY A PROBLEM WITH AN ONLINE STORE

Brandon, a neighbor, asked me to look at a pair of exotic dangling earrings he bought for his wife, Julie, from an internet shop known for its quality products. Her birthday was a week later, and he thought she'd love the multicolored earrings that reminded him of wind chimes blowing in the breeze. However, he was disappointed because the jewelry looked much darker and less sparkly than the ones in the catalog and those shown online.

Julie, his wife, loved wearing glitzy jewelry, but the earrings he showed me looked faded and had more of an antique than a glossy finish. I suggested calling the company and telling them what Brandon told me about the earrings and that I saw for myself, to see if they'd send him a pair that looked more like the ones in the catalog and in their online store.

Brandon hesitated about calling a company to complain about a product. In fact, he never complained about anything. If the food wasn't to his liking in a restaurant, he'd say, "I guess the chef had a bad day" and leave it at that. To complain about the earrings would be out of character for him.

However, I decided to try to convince him. "Knowing Julie, she won't care if the earrings are to her liking because they lack the glitz she loves. But you'll care because you want to please her," I said.

Brandon thought about it and said he'd call the company to tell them that he wanted a replacement. He told the company rep that he didn't think the earrings looked as beautiful as the ones he saw in print or online. The lady on the phone promised she'd send out a pair that was more to his liking. She said she'd include a container in which to return the old ones at no expense to him. The rep sent the earrings special delivery so they arrived the next day. Brandon was more than pleased.

The next day, Brandon knocked on my door to show me the new pair of earrings the company had sent. They were bright and shiny, unlike the dull ones he'd shown me before. The turquoise and gold tones gleamed as they swung back and forth in the breeze like exotic wind chimes fit for a queen.

When Brandon presented the earrings to Julie, she told him how lucky she was to have a husband who gave her such lovely gifts. Brandon was happy that he took my advice to call the company and said that in the future, he won't hesitate to gain satisfaction by voicing his complaint to a company if a product he purchases online or in the store is not up to his standards.

CALL YOUR STATE REP WHEN THINGS GO WRONG

Have you ever called your state representative about something that concerned you locally or nationally? You'll usually find your representative responsive, whether you voted for her or not. Try calling your state rep about local issues, such as your electricity failing repeatedly. This government worker knows how to get access to the right channels to quickly solve your problem. In fact, a state rep solved my problem with constant power outages. The electric company responded quickly to the representative's urgent call and cut down trees in my neighborhood that had stopped the power from getting through.

Your state representative can also fix problems within the province of federal and local government agencies, such as social security and the IRS. Give this valuable resource a call. You'll usually speak to an assistant or intern first. If that person doesn't solve your problem, ask to speak to the representative, who will accelerate your issue in order to reach a resolution to your liking.

Find your state representative's name on the internet under "government officials." Plug "house.gov" into your search engine and then put in your zip code. You'll be surprised about how many ways your state representative can help you. As with all your other efforts in asking for and getting what you want, courtesy and brevity go a long way. Be sure to call rather than text or write so you get a quicker response. The next time you have a problem, consider calling your state representative.

CONTACT AN APPLIANCE COMPANY ABOUT A DEFECTIVE PRODUCT

Calling a company about a defective product usually gets results. Pleasing you is their main concern. A company's best advertisement is word of mouth, and if you like the way they solved your problem and tell people about it, it means better business for them. As mentioned in chapter 2, it's helpful to contact the company's corporate office if you're not satisfied with the response from the vendor who sold you the product.

Once, I found myself with a high-tech refrigerator that stopped functioning about a year after I bought it. The appliance was under warranty, so I called the service warranty department. Their technician failed to remedy the problems, which were serious ones that caused food to spoil. I then called the store where I purchased the refrigerator. To my amazement, they said they were not responsible that the warranty company couldn't repair it properly. In fact, they said, "You bought it; you own it and have to deal with it." I never returned to that store and warned everyone I knew about their lack of cooperation.

My next step was to call the appliance company's corporate office, which said it wasn't their responsibility since the store had sold us an inferior product. I told the representative that they were responsible since they manufactured the product and that I wanted them to repair the refrigerator to our satisfaction or to provide a suitable substitute. They sent out a different repair shop from the warranty company. Like the other shop, this one also failed to repair the refrigerator to my satisfaction.

I took the next step and told the representative that if she didn't take action and replace my old refrigerator with a new one, I'd post my dissatisfaction on social media sites, such as Facebook and Twitter. I made it clear that I'd also share my complaints about the company on review sites such as Yelp. I told her that if she'd change her mind and give me a new appliance, I'd post a retraction on the sites to which I'd sent the negative comments.

Since there were no forthcoming messages from the company, I posted information about my dealings with them on Facebook and Yelp, telling about their unwillingness to rectify the problems I had with their inferior product. After a couple of days, I called the rep and told her to view my comments about her company on the sites. After seeing my comments that were published on the internet sites, the rep said she'd call me back after consulting with her boss. I reminded her that I'd retract my comments if the company decided to change its mind and give me what I wanted, a new refrigerator that worked.

Shortly afterward, she called and said that the company would replace my defective appliance with a brand-new one. She'd also transfer the existing warranty to my new appliance. I thanked her profusely and enjoyed the new refrigerator they delivered the next week for many years to come. I immediately wrote a retraction of my negative remarks about the company and said that they'd rectified the problem and solved the case to my satisfaction.

Throughout my interactions with the appliance store, the warranty company, and the corporate office, I documented my calls by sending letters about what I wanted from each of them. I also wrote down what I did and how the people responded so there was evidence that I placed the calls, what I said, and how they responded. It didn't take long to document the calls and proved helpful every time I talked to the companies on the phone while I worked to refresh my memory and theirs about our interactions in striving to get what I wanted from them.

In my dealings with the corporate office, I used the last step that I rarely have to invoke in getting what I want. Each time you're asking and not receiving to your satisfaction, go up the ladder one step at a time. Reserve this final approach for those rare times you have to resort to doing something extreme for getting the company to respond to your liking.

INSTANT REVIEW

Chapter 6: Contact a Company about a Concern

- Compliment or complain about a company.
- Get refunds from a food company.
- Resolve your issues at the body shop.
- Fix a bad hair day.
- Remedy a problem with an online store.
- Ask your state rep to help.
- Contact an appliance company about a defective product.
- Use the corporate office as your last resort.

7

GET WHAT YOU WANT FROM FRIENDS AND FAMILY

MAKE YOUR CASE USING PROVEN TACTICS

When you want to ask something of family and friends, keep in mind that you'll use some different approaches than you use for contractors and large companies and corporations. For one thing, when it comes to family and friends, you're involved in a close relationship. That can change the dynamics of asking. You know each other's quirks and foibles, so it may be easier in some ways and harder in others.

It's easier because you know already know what makes the people you're asking something of respond positively or negatively. It may pose a challenge because of your past dealings with friends or relatives. They know from prior dealings with you how you're trying to go about getting what you want and will be on the lookout for how you're trying to get them to give in. That said, some of the same tactics you used with strangers or acquaintances will also prove useful in your dealings with family and friends.

For example, positive assertive talk and building rapport with eye contact, coupled with body language, works with most people, whether they're with businesspeople, friends, or relatives. Acting curious about others' feelings and respecting their views will move you toward your goal. Also, using the right words like "I'm hoping you can help me" and "I need you to . . ." go a long way in convincing those close to you to grant your wishes. At the same time, you know exactly how your friends and relatives respond to different approaches you've used in the past, so keep their previous reactions in mind. Use techniques that work; avoid picking one randomly or one that hasn't gotten you anywhere in your past dealings with that person.

Frequently, you find yourself in a situation where you need help from a friend or family member. Often, your natural instincts prompt you to stifle your desire to ask for help. While you believe this person you're close to wants to help, you may think she's too busy to help you, or you don't like imposing on her, or you think she won't do what you want. While in some cases you may be right, in most cases you aren't. You'll never know if friends or family members are willing to help unless you ask.

Drum up the courage to ask, and, more often than not, you'll get what you want from family and friends. All you have to do to get them to listen and respond is make your case convincingly, using proven tactics you believe will work for each specific instance.

CARE FOR THE CAREGIVER

Elyse, a divorced retired teacher, recently moved to her father Mel's home to care for him while he recuperates from heart surgery. When he feels well enough, which she anticipates will take some time, she plans to help him move to an assisted living facility near her apartment so she can visit him frequently.

For now, Elyse bears the full responsibility as her dad's caregiver: driving him to his doctor's appointments, preparing heart-healthy meals, and accompanying him to the rehab center where he exercises twice a week. She found the first couple of weeks manageable, mainly because her father was pleasant and cooperative, but now that reality has set in, he's becoming demanding and impatient with Elyse, totally different from how he acted in the past. He also refuses to think about moving into assisted living, claiming that his daughter is sending him away to "an old people's home" when he and her late mother devoted their whole lives to her and their other two children.

Elyse tried talking to her brother Jacob and sister Sharon about sharing the responsibility for their father's care. Sharon told her that now that her children are in high school she chauffeurs them to all their events and doesn't have a minute to herself. She's also president of the Home and School Association, which takes up at least two evenings a week.

Jacob, Elyse's brother, also absolved himself of doing caregiving chores for their father. He works as a trial lawyer and doesn't get home until 9:00 p.m. most evenings, which gives him little time to devote to his wife and three sons.

Although their dad's insurance financed a home health care aid for a limited time, Jacob offered Elyse money to hire a nursing assistant to help care for their dad when the insurance stops paying. However, given Mel's cantankerous and demanding nature, the nurses the insurance company sent stopped working for the family and left them to fend for themselves. That ended any further assistance from Jacob. Anything that required his presence was not negotiable.

By now, Elyse was at the breaking point. She wanted to help her father, but she couldn't do it alone. She needed her brother and sister's help, which wasn't forthcoming. She didn't want money or advice. She needed their physical presence in their dad's home on at least a weekly basis. She needed them to share the job of driving him to his appointments, and she wanted them to help her convince him to go to assisted living where he could get the specialized care he needed. What could she say to convince her family to help?

She decided to call a family meeting, something she'd never done before. She invited Sharon and Jacob to their dad's home on a Wednesday evening when she knew Sharon would not be involved with the HSA. It was the one day that Jacob took off to enjoy date night with his wife, but he would have to postpone that until next week. Elyse made up her mind she was not going to wait another day to get her siblings to participate actively in their father's care.

That night she prepared a dinner of stuffed tilapia, baked potato, salad, and, keeping her dad in mind, a healthy dessert of fruit with a dollop of whipped cream. Her sister and brother arrived on time, and everyone enjoyed the dinner, except for Mel, who instantly became suspicious that the meeting was about him. After dessert, he told his son and daughters that he was going to his room to watch cable TV so that they could talk about him behind his back as they'd been doing lately. Of course, Jacob and Sharon protested, but out of respect for her dad Elyse wanted to be honest with him.

"Dad, you know I'd never keep anything from you, so I want to tell you that this isn't a regular family gathering. I invited Sharon and Jacob here to talk about their sharing in your care."

"I suspected as much," he said, waving Elyse away as if she were a pesky fly. "I'm going upstairs. Talk all you want. Maybe I'd be better off going to that old people's home."

Mel stormed up to his room unfazed by his kids' attempts to calm him.

Sharon moved toward the stairs to talk to her father, but Elyse stopped her, telling her that the three of them needed to discuss how they could best care for their father.

Sharon reiterated her position that she couldn't spare any time out of her day because of her carpooling and Home and School Association duties. Jacob followed suit by saying that he faced a big trial that he could not trust to his assistant. The case's outcome depended on his presence. The only time he had free was Friday night, which he'd set aside to recoup his energy by spending time with his wife.

Elyse felt it best to tell her brother and sister exactly how she felt without mincing words. She'd listened to them; now it was their turn to listen to her. She told them that she needed their help and that it was nonnegotiable. She was doing all she could to help her father, but she wanted them to participate in his care and help with the move to the assisted living facility when the time came.

She then listened mindfully to her brother and sister without judging them. When she gained her composure to speak, she told her brother that she understood he had a difficult schedule but that she expected him to forgo his night off for a while and stay with their dad so she could do some errands and get some rest. Elyse also told her sister that although she had a heavy schedule driving her kids to their activities and carrying out her duties with the Home and School Association, she expected her to show up at her house two afternoons a week so that she could go food shopping and to her own appointments. She felt that was fair since she carried most of the burden of caring for Mel.

Now for the crucial part: Elyse remained silent for a couple minutes and waited to see how they'd react. When she noticed Jacob squirming in his chair and looking down, she thought he was wrestling with what to do. Her sister's eyes meet hers, so she thought she'd finally decided to help with Mel's care.

Reading their body language helped provide a clue about how they were going to respond. Her sister agreed to help two afternoons a week; she'd get the other parents to assume more of her carpool duties until things calmed down with their dad. When her brother heard that, he said he'd do his best to come over his one free evening, but that she'd have to understand if he couldn't make it. Brother and sisters parted amicably. Both Jacob and Sharon kept their part of the bargain, which made Elyse happy she'd spoken out.

STAND UP; SPEAK OUT

Lily's family has never accepted Jonah since they started dating. Jonah owns a successful auto body shop while his wife earned a doctorate in education and works as a school principal. Jonah always felt that his in-laws thought he wasn't good enough for her, and it turns out he was right in assuming that. Because of their feelings toward him, his wife's parents don't want Jonah to visit them in their home and only want to see Lily when he's not around. In the past, their visits to one another's homes have been rare. This standoff has gone on since they married two years ago, and there doesn't seem to be any solution in sight as both partners have very strong views on the situation.

Lily makes excuses for her parents by telling Jonah they're aging and that she doesn't want to cut them out of her life because she doesn't know how much longer she'll have them. She says they're still her parents and she needs to visit them even though she hates the way they're acting. What choice does she have? If he can't understand that, she doesn't know how to respond.

Jonah thinks that because of the way his in-laws treat him, his wife should cut off all ties with her parents. He thinks that maintaining a relationship with them is a betrayal to him. He needs to find a way to convince Lily that if they are to have a good marriage, she has to make it clear to her parents that he needs to be included in family gatherings and should not be treated like an outcast.

On a sunny Saturday afternoon after a pleasant dinner and conversation at their favorite restaurant, Lily announced that she was going to her parents' the following weekend to celebrate their anniversary. Jonah didn't want to start an argument, especially after the beautiful day they'd spent together, and he was surprised that Lily would bring it up since everything seemed to be going well lately between them.

When Jonah told Lily that they shouldn't discuss it right then, she responded angrily, saying that she'd hoped he would understand that it was an important occasion for her parents who had reserved their favorite restaurant for the occasion and had already invited other family members. She told him she was going no matter what and couldn't understand how he could be so insensitive.

Jonah said that if the issue wasn't resolved soon it could mean serious problems for their marriage and that maybe they should consider a separation, and this wasn't the first time he'd brought it up. For some reason, because of his demeanor and the way he spoke, Lily felt that he meant it this time, so she quickly scrambled to find an answer.

Following mindfulness principles, she put herself in his place. How would she feel if she wasn't welcome in his parents' home? They'd always treated her like a daughter. On second thought, she concluded that he should have the final say in their discussion since he saw himself as the aggrieved party.

Jonah told Lily that he'd reached the end of the line with her going out of her way to placate her parents. They were husband and wife, which according to their marriage vows meant that they were supposed to be first in each other's lives. Jonah told Lily that he wanted her to tell her parents that she'd like to attend their anniversary party but only if he was welcome.

She said that would never happen, given the long-standing hard feelings that they and her husband had for one another. He said that this was a turning point in their relationship and that he'd put up with her giving in to her parents long enough.

Lily knew that he really meant it this time, so she agreed to talk to her parents about Jonah accompanying her to the party. She felt that if she went alone it would mean the end of their relationship. She had to choose, and it was painful.

That afternoon, Lily called her parents and told them that she'd love to attend their anniversary dinner but that she would only attend if Jonah was welcome. She impressed upon them that this had gone on long enough. She loved Jonah and had to put him first, as they always put one another first, ahead of anyone else. She told them that she was coming, and she would bring Jonah. She waited for their response. Her mother said that she wasn't happy about her decision, but if that was the only way Lily would celebrate with them, she'd accept it.

Lily said that there was one more thing. They had to treat Jonah kindly, not like he was an outsider and a pariah, the way they did on the few occasions they both visited. Lily's dad, who participated in the three-way phone conversation, agreed that he would welcome Jonah and be on his best behavior. "It's time this nonsense stopped," he said. Although his wife felt less comfortable with Jonah visiting, to keep the peace with her husband, she agreed to act cordial.

Who knew? Maybe eventually, Lily's parents would fully accept their son-in-law and welcome him into the family. Lily could only hope. This was a start that both she and Jonah could live with.

If things aren't going well between families, it's important to state your position clearly as Jonah did, and if it comes to an ultimatum as it did in this case, that may be the only way to put an end to the problem. In this case, it ushered in a new beginning. After the anniversary party, Jonah regularly accompanied Lily to her parents' home, and he and Lily invited them to their home every so often. Lily's parents now knew that if they wanted to see her, they'd have to include Jonah.

Initially, things felt strained, but in time, Lily's parents gained a new appreciation for Jonah and began to look forward to his visits. In this case, telling rather than asking someone what you want them to do may be the only way to rectify a long-standing problem.

TELL A FRIEND YOU'LL DO THINGS YOUR WAY

Kelly recently gave birth to a beautiful baby girl, her first child. Her friend Sierra, whom she met at the gym a few years ago when they took a Zumba class, keeps hounding her to lose weight. Kelly gained thirty pounds during her pregnancy but, with her part-time job as a computer tech and taking care of her child, has little time to plan and implement a weight loss program. She'd prefer to lose weight on her own at home, and to do it gradually, at her own pace.

Sierra reminds her every day that she needs to start her program or her weight will spiral out of control. Kelly has told her that she understands that it's important for her to lose weight because of high blood pressure and a low energy level since giving birth but that she finds constant reminders from her friend offensive.

For now, Kelly feels comfortable taking short walks; she plans to start a more rigorous program once her daughter gets a little older. However, Sierra won't accept Kelly's way of thinking, which makes Kelly uncomfortable and resentful. She's considering spending less time around Sierra and possibly even ending the friendship. Kelly would like to remain friends with Sierra, but she's not sure how to get her friend to stop making hurtful remarks about her weight. Sierra seems obsessed with it and won't stop bringing it up.

Despite Sierra's efforts to impose her ideas about weight loss on Kelly, she'd proven to be a friend to Kelly in the past. After Kelly gave birth, Sierra brought lunch to her house at least three times a week for the first month, and she volunteered to babysit so her friend could get out of the house to enjoy some free time. Sierra was a friend in many ways, but Kelly considered her preoccupation with her weight a definite deal-breaker.

The next time she and Sierra went out to lunch, Kelly decided to broach the subject. Making herself scarce when Sierra asked her to go out to eat or shopping didn't work, and talking to her gently didn't make her friend any less aggressive in her quest to convince Kelly to begin a weight loss program. She'd thought about it all night and even dreamed about it, but she couldn't find the right words to get Sierra to ease up on her.

Now, sitting in the restaurant watching her friend eat a veggie platter, while she ate onion soup and a burger, made Kelly want to reveal exactly how she felt. She wondered how Sierra would react, but at this point she didn't care. She knew that she wanted to lose weight the way she thought was best, so she told her friend she needed to talk to her about something that they'd discussed before but never resolved.

"A burger and all that cheese on the soup? Really?" Serena said as she eyed Kelly's platter. "Don't you think you're overdoing it? I know that you dislike me saying this, but you're never going to slim down eating that food."

Did Sierra even hear her? By her response, Kelly surmised she didn't. Commenting about her lunch choice was the turning point for Kelly. She took a deep breath and began by telling Sierra how happy she was that they'd remained friends for so many years despite their ups and downs.

(She remembered how many times Sierra had attempted to tell her how to live her life and how she'd shrugged it off, thinking her friend was a more assertive person than she or maybe she was trying to show her concern for her, albeit in a way she didn't appreciate.)

Regardless, Kelly was motivated by her friend's latest display of pushiness at the restaurant to tell her exactly how she felt, knowing that it could possibly end their friendship. It was a chance she had to take.

Sierra asked Kelly where this conversation was going. "Get to the point," she said.

Kelly looked her in the eye and responded that she didn't want Sierra to mention her appearance or anything about losing weight. She didn't want to hear about going on a diet or exercising vigorously while she was still recovering from her pregnancy and birth. She would lose weight on her terms and return to her exercise schedule when she was ready, not when Sierra said she should. She waited for Sierra's response.

Was Sierra at a loss for words? It seemed that way because for a long couple of minutes she didn't say anything. Was she shocked that Kelly stood up to her? Was she angry? What was she thinking? Kelly couldn't gauge her body language because Sierra's expression and gestures didn't change.

After a while, Sierra said, "Thanks for telling me how you feel about this. I only had your interest at heart as I always do. I thought that when you didn't say much about what I said about your losing weight that you were okay with my advice. I know I sometimes give advice to all my friends too freely. I don't think I told you this, but I've lost a few friends over it. I honestly thought you didn't mind my telling you how I felt, and that's why I persisted. Now that I know, I won't say any more about it."

Kelly knew that the conversation was over. She didn't belabor it because she knew that would minimize the impact of her message to Sierra.

It's important to state your position briefly, assertively, and succinctly when you want someone to understand your position and to give you what you want, in this case, to stop giving gratuitous advice.

Postscript: After Kelly aired her position to Sierra, they both enjoyed a brief cooling-off period, during which Sierra didn't call for a couple of weeks. Kelly welcomed the short break. When Sierra finally called and invited her out to a movie, Kelly gladly accepted. Her friend didn't mention weight, diet, or exercise again and granted her the freedom of doing things in her own time and way. In time, Kelly resumed her weight loss program and changed her diet, but solely on her own terms.

ASK FRIENDS FOR HELP WHEN YOU NEED IT

Ivy has a one-year-old baby, Tara, who developed a serious chronic illness that requires constant care. Her husband, Pedro, works as a mechanic and has a second job working for a delivery service. He helps when he's home, but because of his work schedule, he's often away. Ivy took a leave from her job as a retail manager to care for Tara. She'd like to return one day, but full-time care of a special-needs child is expensive, and she's reluctant to leave Ivy until her symptoms become more manageable.

When her friends, Chantel and Angel, found out that Tara had serious health problems, they visited Ivy often and always asked what they could do to help. Although Ivy acted assertively in her management job, she didn't feel comfortable with what she thought of as imposing on her friends. She thought of herself as a person in charge, one who could handle any challenges that came her way, but when it came to asking people in her personal life for help, she searched for the right words to ask but had trouble finding them.

Her challenges caring for Tara were, at times, overwhelming. She often felt alone and isolated in her suburban home where neighbors lived far apart and she had to drive everywhere rather than walk or take public transportation. She saw her friends at her home, but she couldn't meet them at a restaurant because it was difficult caring for Tara in different surroundings that didn't contain her special equipment and medications. However, she was determined to find a plan to find some time for herself so that she could better cope with Tara's issues.

Asking her friends for help was a start. She decided it would be best to talk to Chantel and Angel, her two closest friends, individually and in person, rather than on the phone. She wanted to truly hear what they said and to observe their body language to see if they'd be willing to help her in the ways she needed, which could sometimes involve demanding tasks.

Here is a conversation between Ivy and Chantel, whom she chose to talk to first since they have been friends since high school.

Chantel: Thanks for inviting me for dessert today. I know how busy you are with Tara, so I appreciate your making time to see me.

Ivy: (She observes her friend's body language, which seems open and positive and sees that her tone is caring and receptive.) I'm glad you're here. I'll get straight to the point since I know you have to leave for work soon. I want you to know how much I appreciate your offer to help.

Chantel (looking interested and invested in what Ivy says): I want to know exactly what I can do to help. That's why I asked.

Ivy: Thanks. It would be great if you could help me by stopping by, say, every week or every other week at a time that's good for you. If you could come over for a couple hours to watch Tara so I could go grocery shopping, do some chores, or take a needed break, that would help me in a big way. Tara knows you and enjoys when you play with her, and I'd feel comfortable leaving her with you.

Chantel (getting up from her chair to hug Ivy): Of course I can do that, and I'm sure Angel will want to also. After you talk to Angel, she and I will work out a schedule that works for all three of us.

Ivy: That sounds great. I'm looking forward to getting a break. As you know, taking care of Tara is a full-time job. Maybe I'll function better with some help. I'm glad I asked, and I'm happy you agreed. Thanks, my friend.

Once Ivy talked to Chantel, she knew her conversation with Angel would run smoothly. She'd already had a successful dress rehearsal and had asked for and gotten what she wanted from Chantel. Ivy realized that she had to take the first step to ask for what she wanted. Once she did that, she was on her way to seeing her wishes granted. Ivy used mindfulness techniques of observing tone and body language in the people she asked and made her request briefly, saying exactly what she wanted in her own authentic voice. Voilà, success!

INSTANT REVIEW

Chapter 7: Get What You Want from Friends and Family

- Make your case using proven tactics.
- Care for the caregiver.
- Persist until you get what you want.
- Stand up; speak out for yourself.
- Don't wait to solve a problem.
- Sometimes you need to give an ultimatum.
- Tell a friend you'll do things your way.
- Ask friends for help when you need it.

8

COME OUT ON TOP IN A JOB INTERVIEW

PREPARE FOR YOUR INTERVIEW

When you go on a job interview and take the required tests to qualify for the job, you want the employer to look at your qualifications and weigh your credentials to determine whether you'll be a valuable employee for the company. If you use the techniques in this book when you're thinking about what type of person the employer wants, pay attention to rapport building, and make your points clearly and briefly, you'll move ahead of the other candidates and come out a winner.

The best job candidate always spends time preparing for the interview by researching the type of person the organization would most likely choose for the position. Learn the facts and figures about the company by looking on the internet under the company's name so that you're knowledgeable about the company before you apply for the job.

Study the organization's mission statement to see what their goals for the company include. For example, if you're applying to a school district for a teaching job, see what they expect of their employees. A large urban school district includes empowering students to gain "their full intellectual and social potential" in its mission statement. It also mentions making students "lifelong learners." If you're applying for a job in this school district, state in your interview how you'll specifically fulfill the goals in their mission statement.

In addition to empowering students to reach for their "full potentials, both intellectually and socially," it's important in a teaching job to individualize instruction and to pay attention to students' unique learning styles to help them learn the way they learn best. If you want to help them develop their social potentials, you'll offer to provide learning activities that would engage them with other students in the class and to hone their conversation skills so that they can express themselves clearly and effectively. During your interview, refer to the company (in this case, school) mission statement to let the evaluators know that you did your homework regarding your prospective place of employment. It helps if you give specific examples of how you plan to implement the mission statement.

EXPRESS YOURSELF WELL IN WRITING AND SPEECH

Certain positions require both a written and an oral component in their interview. For the written segment, be sure you're aware of grammar rules and conventions of good writing style. For example, recently the dictionary added the singular *they* to accommodate people who do not choose to identify themselves as *he* or *she*. Most style manuals now approve the singular *they* for all segments of society to help writers avoid using *he* or *she* or having to alternate these two pronouns among paragraphs or pages.

Here's an example of the singular *they*: Each candidate must bring *their* best speaking and writing ability when *they* (instead of *he* or *she*) go to the job interview. In this sentence the antecedent (word to which *they* refers) is candidate, a singular noun. Some people still choose to use inclusive (nonsexist) language the traditional way, but they will probably use the new way as time goes by.

To make your writing look professional for a prospective employer, always choose the simpler, more concise word; spell correctly; and avoid long paragraphs because short ones are easier on readers' eyes.

Although some jobs require a written segment, all interviews use an oral interview to help the employer get a good idea of how you speak and to assess the quality of your ideas. For this reason, remember to avoid verbal tics, vocal fry, and speak strongly and directly to make your point (see chapter 1). Pack a lot of what you want to say in a few words since most employers appreciate workers who can express themselves clearly and get to the point without wasting words.

DRESS THE PART

Even if the company you choose to work for allows informal clothing style, dress so that you look professional and authoritative. If employees don't wear neckties or high heels, you may want to follow their lead; however, in many cases, you'll want to dress the way you would if you wanted to command respect.

Colors give messages to prospective employers about the image you wish to project. Many people who go to job interviews wear drab, neutral colors, but if you want to stand out from the crowd, wear (at least for part of your outfit) a bright color like red or purple, such as a red tie or jacket. Red is a power color and gives off a visual clue that you're energetic and will give your best to the job. Royal blue is another shade that helps you show strength and power.

Sometimes wearing your favorite colors will help you make the best impression because those are the ones that make you feel most relaxed and comfortable. Stay away from drab and dingy shades. If you're a wild dresser, think about dressing more conservatively and less flamboyantly. Consider the impression you want to make and how to make it in the best way possible.

ANTICIPATE INTERVIEW QUESTIONS

Before you go on your interview, take the time to anticipate questions. Think about what's current in the news related to your job, and jot down some ideas about questions you think the interviewer will ask related to what's happening in the country or the world. When I applied for an administrative job in my school district, I knew that many people were pondering what they could do to help solve the drug problem. It was, and still is, a major national concern and posed a challenge in our urban school district. When preparing for the test, I researched and studied specific things I could do to help remedy the problem as it pertained to the schools.

As it turned out, the person who wrote the written component of the interview asked this and other questions I'd anticipated beforehand. Think about what's going on nationally and locally that may apply to your prospective job, and research the topic. Write brief talking points you'll use in your interview. Even if the written and/or oral components of the test don't contain the questions you choose, you'll get practice formulating logical and convincing responses to your questions.

When you answer the questions in the oral interview, repeat part of the question back to the questioner. It helps you stay on the topic, and it shows the interviewer you're doing your best to address the question. In your study sessions for the oral section of the interview, you'll also want to anticipate generic questions the evaluator may ask. After you think about sample interview questions (ones commonly used and ones you think of), practice in a mock interview by yourself or with a friend who you believe will give you an honest assessment of your performance.

Here are some examples of types of questions the interview may ask you and some ideas about how to answer them. Be sure to inject your unique personality into your answers. Your interviewers want to learn as much as they can about you.

- **Tell me about yourself.** When you address this one, explain who you are, and talk about what you consider your best accomplishment in the workplace. Show by example how you work well with others and how you're a good listener. This is not a time to highlight your faults but to emphasize your positive traits.
- **Why do you want this job?** Speak honestly about why the job interests you and what you've done in the past to prepare you for it. Talk about the challenges and rewards of the job as you see them.
- **What are you passionate about?** Discuss things in your life (relationships, hobbies, ideas) that intrigue and excite you. Talk specifically about how you'll bring this passion to the job. Avoid getting into personal areas such as politics that may evoke controversy. Keep it light and upbeat.
- **Why are you leaving your present position to seek a new one?** Speak about looking for a new opportunity to use your talents to their best advantage. Address opportunities for advancement within the new company without focusing on money; you can discuss that later, after landing the job. Talk about the excitement you experience about working for this new company.
- **What are your weaknesses?** Be careful with this one as you want the interviewer to perceive you as honest and realistic in your self-assessment, but, at the same time, you don't want him to see you as

critical of yourself or lacking in self-esteem. Instead, talk about a trait you'd genuinely like to improve and how you're going about accomplishing that. Address a couple of specific things you're doing now to change your weaknesses into strengths.

USE BODY LANGUAGE TO ITS BEST ADVANTAGE

When striving for a successful job interview, what you don't say is as important, if not more so, than what you do say. How can you ensure that your body language imparts a message that you're a strong, confident candidate? It's important that you act mindfully curious as your interview progresses about how the evaluator perceives you.

You can often tell by looking at positive signs such as a warm smile on her part or nodding when you say something that meets her approval. If you don't think she's giving you positive feedback in body language and/or speech, you can change your approach. How can you project body language that will back up your answers and help you get the job you want? Be sure to look your interviewer in the eye, but don't overdo it as it may make her uncomfortable, and keep your body language positive and open rather than closed and constricted.

People gravitate toward people who act like them, but if you overdo mimicking a person's gestures, it may backfire, causing him not to take you seriously, or make him think you're trying to manipulate him into giving you the job. Imitate your interviewer's body language, but be subtle about it. Do it in a way that you're using body language as he does, but don't act like an exaggerated caricature of how he moves and acts. If he leans toward you, lean slightly toward him. Mirror his gestures, but do it so it doesn't look like you're purposefully doing it.

Use your hands occasionally to emphasizes a point you're making, but avoid doing it too frequently as it may distract the person asking the questions.

ASK THE RIGHT QUESTIONS

It's important to answer the interviewer's questions to the best of your ability so that you'll convince her to choose you for the job. It's equally important to ask the right questions. Here's a transcript of an interview for an assistant principal's job in an urban high school. Take note of the last section in which the evaluators, the district superintendent, the high school principal, and a Home and School Association representative give the candidate a chance to ask *them* questions.

Cast of characters: Lionel Brooks, applicant for the job of assistant principal at Kennedy High School; Dr. Thomas Parker, district superintendent; Dr. Anna Price, principal of Kennedy High School; and Ms. Sofia Garcia, president, Home and School Association.

Lionel, the applicant, passed the written exam for assistant principal with a high grade. Now he faces the oral committee for the final part of the interview.

Dr. Parker: Lionel, we'd like to welcome you to this interview today. I'm Dr. Parker, district superintendent. This is Dr. Price, principal of Kennedy, whom you already know. Ms. Garcia is here to represent the parent-teacher organization. (Looking each of the interviewers in the eye and smiling, Lionel shakes hands with each interviewer.)

Dr. Parker: Lionel, I commend you for your high score on the written test. I want you to feel comfortable during the interview. Feel free to ask questions when we finish asking ours. It's often during this time that we learn the most about our applicants.

Lionel: Thanks, Dr. Parker. I look forward to answering your questions and asking the committee questions.

Dr. Parker (smiling): Then let's get started. Can you tell us about yourself?

Lionel: I've gone to the schools in this district all my life and graduated from Kennedy High School. It's always been my dream to work there because all the teachers I've had were dedicated and caring. In fact, they inspired me to become an English teacher.

Dr. Price: You teach in our School for the Performing Arts. What do you consider your greatest accomplishment there?

Lionel: I wrote and produced a musical that we performed for the community. I'm proud to say it got rave reviews in the press. After that, the governor invited the cast to his residence for a special performance. That was the highlight of my career, although teaching there every day was an adventure for me. The students' enthusiasm for performing motivated and inspired me to do my best. I'm grateful that they taught me as much as I taught them.

Ms. Garcia: I love to see a teacher who enjoys the job as much as you do, Lionel. I was fortunate to see that performance, and I'd put it on a par with a show at the Walnut Street Theater.

Lionel: Thanks, Ms. Garcia.

Ms. Garcia: I'd like to ask what you see as your greatest personal strength.

Lionel: I see my greatest strength as my ability to motivate students to do their best every day, whether it's learning about how to improve their writing, express themselves clearly in speech, or perform their best in the shows we put on. I also see myself as a performer in that a teacher is always onstage, working to help students achieve excellence. If I'm excited and passionate about my job, they will be too.

Dr. Parker: What interests you most about this job?

Lionel: I see the assistant principal's job as an opportunity to influence more people than I did as a teacher. Part of my duties in this job include working in the discipline office. In that capacity, I can help kids turn their lives around and help set them on the right path if they're having trouble in school with academics or social interactions. When I observe teachers' performances and evaluate them, I'll give them practical advice about how to handle behavior problems and how to reach a wider group of students by honing their teaching skills. To sum it up, this job will present new challenges to me that I'll gladly welcome. I'm ready for the job, and I'm excited about becoming an assistant principal and helping make Kennedy a rewarding experience for kids, teachers, and parents.

Dr. Price: Knowing how much you love your job here at Kennedy, I'd like to ask why you're leaving your current job. As you probably know, and I definitely do as principal, being an administrator presents its own unique problems. You'll open yourself up to more negativity than you've experienced as a teacher here at Kennedy Performing Arts. You'll deal with fights and bullying, some uncooperative parents, and me always breathing down your neck, holding you accountable when your ideas backfire. So, Lionel, why are you leaving your comfortable job to be thrown into the lions' den?

Lionel (relaxed and smiling, making eye contact with Dr. Price and other members of the panel): All I can say, Dr. Price, is that I'm ready to go to the next level. I have years of experience dealing with fights and kids bullying. Kids are always going to be kids, and we have to meet them where they are and go from there to solve these problems.

As for uncooperative parents, I've met a few as a teacher, but once they know I have their children's best interest at heart, they're willing to work with me to make things better for their kids. As for you holding me accountable when my ideas don't pan out, I'm ready for that too. I've always held myself accountable if I make a mistake, and I'm willing to start over if I don't do it right the first time.

Dr. Price: Thanks, Lionel. I've known you a long time, but this interview helped me and all of us get to know you a little better, and it was a pleasure. I'll turn the final question over to our superintendent, Dr. Parker.

Dr. Parker: For our last question, I'd like to ask if you have any questions for us, Lionel.

Lionel (thinking a moment and making eye contact with all of them): I have one question, Dr. Parker.

All the panel members look up at him with interest.

Lionel: What do you look for in your ideal candidate? I'd like to hear from each one of you.

Ms. Garcia: That's an easy one for me. I'd want to see an assistant principal who will make parents feel comfortable if they need to contact you about their child.

Lionel: I'll make parents feeling comfortable a priority when I become an assistant principal. I'll make them feel welcome at our annual back-to-school night by introducing myself and laying out my goals for their kids, which involves helping them grow in their subject-matter knowledge and social skills. I'll let them know that if they ever want to talk, I'm always here for them. I also plan to send out a parents' newsletter over the web on an as-needed basis.

Dr. Price: My ideal candidate would be one who's willing to put in all the time it takes to get the job done, an assistant principal who doesn't work by the clock.

Lionel: Dr. Price, as you know, I've often stayed at school extra time when the job called for it. Sometimes, as a teacher and administrator I have to put in more time to get the job done. Some things can't wait until tomorrow. When I'm chosen for the job, I'll do everything, and then some, to give it one hundred percent. Of course, I'm realistic and will also allow myself time to exercise, have a social life, and keep fit. If I live a well-balanced life, while at the same time giving my best efforts to the job, I'll be an excellent assistant principal.

Dr. Parker: My ideal candidate would bring to the assistant principal's job energy and creativity.

Lionel: Anyone who knows me can tell you that I have boundless energy. I coach the softball team and write, produce, and stage plays for the community. Last year we performed at the governor's home. I like to think of myself as indefatigable, or, in plain English, a tireless worker. Creativity is my main selling point for this job. I love to find new ways to help kids, parents, and teachers work as a team to meet a common goal, to help everyone learn and grow together for their own betterment and that of Kennedy High School. In closing, I want to say that I believe I can meet your expectations in all the areas we discussed.

Dr. Parker: Thank you, Lionel, for your perceptive answers. We'll get back to you and the other candidates within a week. I must say that this is the first time anyone I've interviewed asked a question that told us all we needed to know about how he or she planned to carry out their duties.

Lionel: I'd like to thank all members of the panel for giving me the chance to interview for this position at my alma mater. I've enjoyed the experience.

Lionel ended the interview and took control of the process with a novel approach, asking the panel what characteristics their ideal candidate would possess. Then he responded by saying how he would meet those expectations. I consider a question like this one to be an excellent way to end an interview for any type of position in the public or private sector. My aunt and mentor, Dr. Monica Uhlhorn, a retired school superintendent, told me about using the technique, and I received two job offers because of it. Think about using it when you participate in your interview.

Postscript: Because Lionel used the mindfulness principles of curiosity, positive speech, and body language during the interview, the committee chose him for the assistant principal's job. If, like Lionel, you keep an open mind and allow yourself to enjoy the interview, you'll project that positivity throughout the process and give yourself a good chance landing your dream job.

INSTANT REVIEW

Chapter 8: Come Out on Top in a Job Interview

- Prepare for your interview.
- Study the organization's mission statement.
- Express yourself well in writing and speech.
- Dress the part.
- Anticipate interview questions.
- Look up common interview questions.
- Stage a mock interview.
- Use body language to its best advantage.
- Ask the right questions.

9

ASK AND RECEIVE ON THE JOB

GET A COWORKER TO STOP BOTHERING YOU

No matter how much you enjoy your job, it's inevitable that sometime you'll deal with a toxic coworker. These annoying workers fall into many different categories, but they all have one thing in common: the ability to make their coworkers miserable. Sometimes they're not aware of it, but most of the time they are because people in the workplace make themselves scarce when they're around.

What works for you when a coworker barrages you with endless questions about your personal life or gives details that you'd rather not know about hers? Whatever techniques you use when dealing with this person who's hell-bent on making your life miserable, be brief and businesslike when interacting with her. Better yet, avoid contact as much as possible. Often these types of people act aggressive and pushy, so you have to beware of too much contact as they create untold stress on the job.

Once you respond to these people, you'll get caught up in their drama and they'll never give you peace. On the contrary, they'll wait for you at your desk to regale you with embarrassingly personal details about their lives both on and off the job. They're also adept at trying to pry information about your life on the job and your personal life that you don't want to share with anyone but family and close friends.

With pesky, bothersome coworkers like this, the best path to take is to disassociate yourself from them and keep your distance.

HANDLE A KNOW-IT-ALL EFFECTIVELY

Know-it-alls are another type of toxic coworker that you need to avoid. These aggressive people think they know everything and have the right answer to every problem. They love to give unsolicited advice and won't stop pressuring you until you come around to their way of thinking and carrying out tasks in the workplace. If you don't, watch out. They'll label you as inflexible or bad-mouth you in other ways to others.

If you attend a group meeting with a know-it-all where the boss presides, this person will likely brag about his accomplishments. In fact, self-adulation is his most prominent trait. You can tell by the looks on the other attendees' faces that they'd rather be anywhere but at this meeting watching Mr. Know-It-All congratulate himself.

A know-it-all is usually also the first one to speak out and impose her ideas on other members of the team without listening to other associates' opinions. If other people's ideas do not agree with hers, she'll be the first to find a reason they won't work. In her mind, only her ideas count and will bring the company more accolades because she alone knows everything when it comes to the business.

If you're a manager, it's best to wrest control away from people like this as they tend to be big talkers at meetings even though they usually have nothing substantial to say. Don't give him a chance to dominate the meeting. Say something like "Does anyone have any of their own ideas to add?" or "Since we're pressed for time, I'd like to hear from someone else." Always avoid encouraging him to continue his long-winded speeches. Watch the body language and eye cues of other associates attending the meeting, and take it seriously.

If you're a coworker, avoid the know-it-all as much as possible and don't engage her in lengthy conversations. Be civil but not overly friendly unless you're open to hearing her pontificate about her ideas. If she persists in telling you about her thoughts about transforming the company (or your life) to her way of thinking, say thank you and move on without any further discussion.

Brevity often works well in cutting off these menaces to the workplace. If it doesn't, politely ask the know-it-all to cease and desist without embellishing your request or giving in to anger. Don't recite a long list of reasons about why you reject his ideas or proposals. Then walk away, and have the best last word—silence.

DEAL WITH COMPLAINERS AND MALCONTENTS

If you deal with complainers and malcontents in your workplace, you know how they can sap your energy and that of their coworkers. If you're in management, you may find it particularly taxing because there's nothing you can do to placate them. They complain about the people they work with, their working conditions, or about what you haven't done to help them. The best thing you can do is to listen to their negativity for as short a time as possible and not let them ramble on enough for it to affect your mental or physical health.

If their whining and complaining becomes more frequent or intense, and you can't do anything to change their way of dealing with problems, refer them to Human Resources. If their negativity gets in the way of their performance or adversely influences others who try their best to do their jobs, convince them to seek other employment. If they refuse and persist in their counterproductive behavior, suggest that they seek a more suitable job since they're unhappy with their current work situation. If it gets to the point where you consider terminating their employment, you'll need to document their performance and behavior on the job. They may seek legal advice, so ensure that all the measures you take to deal with their issues are within legal boundaries.

If you're a coworker who works closely with people who constantly complain or whine about the company or carrying out their duties, or who refuse to cooperate, tell them you understand, but that this is the way it's done here. Emphasize that it's uncomfortable for you to work with people who never have anything positive to say. If they persist in cutting into the quality of your work experience, talk to your immediate supervisor. If the supervisor doesn't help, go up the management ladder until someone assists you in changing your work environment to your satisfaction.

BEWARE OF OFFICE GOSSIPS

Office gossips can hurt your reputation among those who work with you and your superiors. The best way to deal with them is to take the path of least resistance and avoid them. If they persist in talking to you about others in the workplace, say something like this: "I hope you understand that I don't talk about people, and I don't want to hear others do it either."

When dealing with any problems in the workplace, be assertive, straight-forward, and direct. Above all, be brief and don't prolong the conversa-tion. Walk away before the person has a chance to respond. If she persists in bad-mouthing another worker, say, "I don't want to hear it," or "I'm not interested."

Suppose you're a manager and someone wants to reveal personal things about someone you supervise, for example, that he's cheating on his spouse, or that she has a drinking problem, or something else that is not anyone else's business. Tell the gossiper that you aren't interested in hearing personal details about coworkers' lives, and shut down the con-versation quickly. If she persists in confiding rumors about the other worker, tell her that this is a workplace where you expect employees to act professional and that you aren't interested in hearing what she's say-ing.

If you work closely with someone who spreads gossip, deal with him as little as possible, and when you do, act businesslike and professional. Never reveal anything personal to him as he may spread the information to others. If the situation intensifies, talk to your superior and make it clear that you do not want to be involved in what the person is doing.

If privy to office gossip, avoid the temptation to spread rumors. It hurts your reputation at work, and it takes away from your rating as an employee. At all times, be professional and don't discuss people's per-sonal lives with others.

STAVE OFF OFFICE BULLIES AND HARASSERS

If a bully has ever bothered you at work, you know the pain it causes. The sense of loneliness, alienation, and emotional distress can cause psycho-logical and physical reactions. That's why you should do everything you can to get the bully/bullies to stop.

Workplace bullying often occurs because of jealousy. One or more workers find ways to harass an employee because she's singled out by management as an excellent, dependable worker. She may receive pro-motions or awards from the company or simply be thought of highly and given extra compensation or recognition from her superiors. This type of bullying may be subtle (shunning by employees at lunch and during social functions) or vicious and outright (spreading rumors and hateful messages about the employee via social media and the internet). It may also involve telling the person's boss things that aren't true about her performance to make her look incompetent and foolish.

If you find out that people are bullying you because of jealousy, speak to your superior and tell him honestly what you think and why you believe it. If doing that doesn't stop their behavior, meet with Human Resources and file a complaint. As in the other cases mentioned in this chapter, have no interaction with those who try to make your life miserable.

Most cases of bullying involve spreading gossip and malicious rumors about the victim throughout the office and on the internet. This often happens with those who are in some way different from the people bullying them. Some may be different in their appearance, sexual orientation, or religious beliefs.

Disgruntled workers sometimes also single out people who have physical or psychological differences from the workers bullying them. In a used car dealership, two women who worked in the office tormented Jessie, an older woman with a facial rash and the blue/black fingers that accompany an immunological disorder, Raynaud's disease. While the receptionists in the office worked together as a team, two of the other ladies didn't include Jessie in after-hours events that their clique held, such as happy hour or bowling. Jessie sat alone at her desk while the other women ate in the cafeteria and brought in cakes and cookies they'd brought from home. They also talked behind her back and ridiculed her appearance, calling her "ghoul" and "alien" because of her blue fingers.

At the urging of an acquaintance who worked in a nearby department, Jessie spoke to her boss and Human Resources, who did all they could to help stop the harassment, including talking to the women involved. The mistreatment stopped for a short time—until the intimidators found out that there was no penalty meted out other than a warning to stop treating their coworker shabbily.

An acquaintance in the next department urged Jessie to file a complaint with the Equal Employment Opportunity Commission (EEOC). This government agency contacted the company and told the manager and Human Resources department that they wanted to create a plan that would let this worker live a peaceful life, rather than come to work every day to face psychological intimidation that could worsen her health condition.

They would also engage in a mediation with the company's general manager if necessary. It never came to that because the general manager, along with the company's manager and Human Resources, quickly complied and formally reprimanded the women who bullied Jessie. They were all put on suspension for a week. After that, these women never bothered her again.

They didn't associate with her or invite her to after-work events, but that pleased Jessie immensely. Management issued a termination warning if the women bullied her again. Although they had the right to legal counsel, they would find it hard to find another job since what they did would go on their records. Jessie and the lady who was incensed at how the bullies treated her began socializing after work and became good friends.

Always speak out if you're bullied on the job or if you see someone at work mistreated. If one person in management doesn't help you, another will. If they dismiss your requests to stop workplace bullying, contact Human Resources and then a government agency, like the EEOC or the Human Relations Commission.

GET EMPLOYEES TO COOPERATE

If you're a manager, you need to know the best way to get employees to cooperate and get the job done. Whenever you can, include employees in making decisions for your department. Be curious and willing to listen when they pose objections to your ideas about running your department. "Tell me more" or "I want to know what you think about the new policy before I implement it" are helpful phrases you can use to show employees you're open to their suggestions. You can also say, "I value your opinions and will consider them when I put the new policies into effect." Delegate wisely to those you most trust with important tasks, and participate with workers in achieving goals you set for them. People learn best by example rather than by always hearing someone tell them what to do.

Treat workers as equals, and you'll find them more willing to cooperate and move the company forward. Criticizing and berating workers for their shortcomings often has the opposite effect. Show them you're willing to meet them halfway in making decisions and that you're willing to listen to any problems that arise when they face challenges carrying out their duties. Listen to what they have to say as a group and one on one. Solve any problems with their best interests and that of the company in mind. Your team will be more productive and willing to cooperate if they have a say in doing what you tell them.

If you want your employees to become team players, treat them with respect. Gaining their respect means acting confident but humble. Don't hesitate to admit when you've made a mistake. Employees will regard you as more human because you're willing to learn from your mistakes. You can also build respect and set a good example by being the best employer you can be and by holding high expectations for those you supervise to do the same. You can't expect everyone to like you, but you can do specific things to gain their respect. It pays off in the long run in greater productivity and in gaining a cohesive department that works as a unit toward its goals.

Be sure each team member's role is clearly defined. If an employee isn't sure of his responsibilities, speak to him privately, outlining his duties and putting them in writing. When an employee starts a job, walk him through his duties and answer questions he has as a new employee. A new person on the job may be overwhelmed at first and will need a great deal of guidance. Team him with a mentor who's been in a similar position whom he can readily approach with any questions as he learns the intricacies of the job.

When someone does something well, offer specific praise, such as "I like the way you got that job done. I can always depend on you to do it right," or "Thanks for being part of our team. I appreciate your efforts to work well with others to make our company run smoothly."

If workers have disagreements, encourage them to find the answers themselves instead of telling them to do things your way. Getting involved, unless the problem escalates, often complicates the issue, making it more difficult to find a common ground. However, if you see a worker being mistreated by a coworker, intervene immediately, and do your best to solve the problem. If it worsens, refer the parties to Human Resources, and continue to work toward a resolution.

Don't listen to gossip about other employees. If a person persists in talking about others, don't buy into the conversation. Work with slackers or unmotivated people to encourage better performance. There will always be somebody who needs a little push.

Use your intuition and logic to help you make the best decisions for your company and for those you employ. Be yourself at all times, and put yourself in an employee's place if a problem comes up. Never be too proud to say, "I don't know the answer, but we'll work together to find a solution."

KNOW HOW TO ASK FOR A RAISE

Francesca has worked at Bella Roma restaurant for five years, first as a server, and then as a hostess. She assumed additional duties in her hostess role, such as training new waitstaff, seating customers, and ensuring quality food and service. She's asked for a raise for the last two years. Matteo, the owner, told her he'd love to give her one but that he isn't making enough of a profit lately to justify it. Food delivery by competing restaurants and meal delivery services, where people cook their own meals, is starting to cut into Matteo's business. He wonders how he can afford to give Francesca a raise, but he wants to keep her as an employee, which poses a dilemma for him.

Francesca decides that she can't wait any longer to ask for what she wants. Is her intuition kicking in, and is she right that this is a good time to ask for a raise? Before asking for a raise, Francesca does some research. She thinks about when Matteo feels his best, when his mood is bright and positive. Monday is always a difficult day because he orders food for the week (which she helps with), and he doesn't have a spare moment.

Tuesday or Wednesday would be better days because the restaurant doesn't draw much of a lunch crowd on those days. The other days, customers line up in the lobby, so that wouldn't work either. Francesca decides on Tuesday because Matteo won't feel as pressured as he would on the other days. In fact, Tuesday is the day that the two of them enjoy a leisurely lunch in the dining room to taste test new items and have a glass of red wine while the assistant manager takes over their duties.

Here is a conversation between Francesca and Matteo:

Francesca: The dinner was superb, Matteo, as was the wine.

Matteo: Thanks. I'm glad we could enjoy it today. One of the perks of the job—right?

Francesca: (She pauses a moment to key in on Matteo's mood. When she determines by his body language that he's in a good mood, she sets the stage for asking for what she wants.) It's a big perk, one I'm grateful for, along with this job. You know how much I enjoy working here.

Matteo (smiling): I sense a question coming. I know when you get that look in your eyes, you're about to ask for something.

Francesca: As a matter of fact, you guessed right. You know me well, Matteo.

Matteo: Before we get back to work, tell me what's on your mind. I think I have an idea.

Francesca: We've spoken about it before. I'd like to ask you for a raise. You've increased my duties, and I love doing them to make Bella Roma the five-star restaurant that everyone loves. As you know, we won the People's Choice Awards five years in a row.

Matteo (nodding): Mainly because of you, Francesca. Everyone loves you—the employees, the cooks, the customers. My business wouldn't have flourished if it weren't for you, and I appreciate that. I'd love to give you a raise, but, as you know, competition from those two new bistros they've built in this area and people using takeout services have cut into my profits.

Francesca: I hear you, Matteo, and I understand perfectly. However, suppose I found a way for you to give me the raise without feeling the sting of taking away from your profits.

Matteo (leaning forward): I'm interested. Tell me more.

Francesca: How about if you give me a raise that we both consider fair, but you could do it in increments instead of giving me the raise all at once.

Francesca pauses to gauge Matteo's interest in what she's proposing and to consider if his body language looks receptive.

Matteo: (He leans forward in his chair, so his body language appears open and receptive to her.) Go on, I'm listening.

Francesca: You could increase my holiday bonus this year, along with a raise that we negotiate. Next year, you can give me another raise, but hold off on paying half of it for six months.

Matteo: It's starting to sound more manageable than having to come up with the money all at once.

Francesca: I don't like to bring this up, but Aldo, the owner of Nonna's Ristorante, offered me a good salary, substantially more than what I earn here, to work as a night manager for him. I want to stay with you, Matteo. You're like family to me, and we work well together, but I need to make a better salary. As a single mom, it's hard to make ends meet, and with Alyssa starting college next year, my financial obligations will increase.

Matteo: I certainly do not want that little weasel Aldo to steal you away from me. Let's sit down tomorrow and work out the details of what we'd both consider a fair amount for a raise and how to make it work for both of us.

Francesca: Thanks, Matteo. I knew you'd be willing to listen and help make things better for me.

Francesca got the raise she asked for because she appealed to her boss's sense of fairness. She also used mindfulness techniques to get her wishes granted. Francesca made sure to choose an opportune time to talk to Matteo. During the process, she acted curious about how he processed her request with his words and body language. She used a brief silence to give Matteo time to think about what she said and to consider her proposal.

Francesca also put herself in her boss's shoes when he explained why he hadn't previously given her a raise by saying, "I hear you, Matteo, and I understand perfectly." Then she quickly offered solutions. She used magic words like "I need." Francesca briefly and succinctly explained why she needed a raise at this time. She didn't tell a long, sad story to evoke pity but explained her financial need in a straightforward way. All these factors worked together to help Francesca ask for what she wanted and get it.

INSTANT REVIEW

Chapter 9: Ask and Receive on the Job

- Get a coworker to stop bothering you.
- Handle a know-it-all effectively.
- Deal with complainers and malcontents.
- Beware of office gossips.
- Avoid the temptation to spread rumors.
- Stave off office bullies and harassers.
- Get employees to cooperate.
- Know how to ask for a raise.

10

ASK AND RECEIVE IN THE EDUCATIONAL ARENA

KNOW THE RIGHT PERSON TO ASK

The educational arena is one of the most important venues for asking and receiving on a daily basis. Employees, parents, and students need to ask in precisely the right way to get what they want to help their schools to run smoothly. These different factions need to work together to ensure that everything gets done in an auspicious and timely manner.

Academic department heads depend upon the principal to grant them funds for books, supplies, and additional employees to keep class size manageable. Also, parents need to talk to assistant principals and counselors if their child encounters a problem with a teacher. Students want to know how to ask their teachers about a poor grade and what they can do to remedy the situation. They also need to consult with their school counselor if they want to know how to perform better academically. Finally, parents can turn to their school boards if they have a special request that no one else in the system can grant.

ASK FOR BOOKS, EQUIPMENT, AND SUPPLIES

You're the science department head in an inner-city high school where books and supplies often don't meet the students' needs. Your principal tells the staff at a faculty meeting that there's little money for new textbooks this year. The textbooks you're using for your science class are outdated and contain misinformation in light of updated scientific theories. You're concerned that the principal won't give any more money to your department because she's already started distributing the money among the various departments. You learned from a colleague in the math department that teachers received new textbooks last year, while the books for your department are ten years old. You decide to appeal to the principal about acquiring the books you need before approaching the union, your last resort. What should you say to make your case so that you receive the needed books?

You decide to approach Ms. Brown, the principal, on a Friday during your lunch period because that's when she's free for a few minutes. Although she looks frazzled from an encounter with the dean of discipline about a student who threatened another student whom he believes stole his jacket, she asks you to sit down.

You explain that the teachers in the science department are using antiquated textbooks and that students won't be able to pass their standardized tests without learning the latest information. Mainly, they won't learn about the latest scientific discoveries that will set them apart from the students in neighboring school districts.

Ms. Brown explains that there isn't any more money this year as she's already drawn up an allocation plan for the money that she believes is fair to all academic departments.

You mention that other departments have new textbooks and that yours is the only one using outdated ones. Ms. Brown counters that the reason for this is that you decided last year to spend your allotment on equipment and supplies. You tell her you did that because your students needed new microscopes and lab experiment equipment. The principal tells you that she understands the problem, but she can't spare any more funds at this time.

You know you have to think quickly to get money for these books, because by Ms. Brown's body language and short manner you know she isn't willing or able to think of a way to give you what you want.

"I have an idea," you say. "I know you don't like borrowing money, but can you count my new textbook purchases against my next year's allotment? I'd have less to spend then on supplies and equipment, but I already have enough from my order last year."

Ms. Brown says that won't be possible, but she praises you for your persistence in lobbying for what the students need. After a few minutes of silence, she says she has some extra money in an emergency fund and that she could get the money for your books from there, although there may not be enough to give every student a book to take home. You thank the principal but realize that sometimes students will need to sign out the books on a rotating basis so they're able to do their homework and study for tests. Ms. Brown thanks you for understanding, and you're happy that you have new textbooks for your department.

REQUEST HELP FOR A PROBLEM WITH YOUR CHILD'S TEACHER

Jayne, a parent, wants to request a class change for her son Braxton, who performs poorly in Spanish. He says that Mr. Cordón, his teacher, speaks too fast and he can't understand him, no matter how hard he tries. Jayne tells Ms. Robbins, the assistant principal, her problem.

Ms. Robbins says that she can't change Braxton's class at this point because the other Spanish classes are filled to capacity. She refers her to Dr. Fleishman, the school counselor, and says that the counselor will work as an intermediary to help solve Braxton's problem in Spanish class. Jayne tells Ms. Robbins that Braxton has a newly diagnosed hearing impairment that makes it difficult for him to process different sounds, especially in Spanish. When people speak rapidly, he can't understand what they say. He wears a hearing aid, but that wouldn't help with someone who speaks quickly like his teacher.

The counselor sets up a meeting with Jayne, her son Braxton, Ms. Robbins, and the teacher. In the meeting, Jayne explains her problem: "My son has a hearing impairment, and we're trying to find a way for him to succeed in Spanish. This is the only class keeping him off the honor roll, and it's important for him to make it. He has a problem with the class he's in because he has specific needs."

Mr. Cordón asks for ways he can help Braxton. Braxton's mother says, "You can speak more slowly and give my son some extra help so that he can do better. I hope you can help us." Mr. Cordón says that he wishes he'd been aware of the problem at the outset, but Jayne points out that her son is shy about his hearing problem and doesn't want to say anything about it. The teacher says he'd be glad to speak more slowly and to give Braxton extra help after school whenever he needs it. The assistant principal has also arranged for an in-school hearing professional to help Braxton in his Spanish class since that is the only class that presents a problem.

When Jayne asks the teacher if Braxton will receive a poor grade for the first report period, the assistant principal suggests that Mr. Cordón give him a "withheld" until the next report period. That way, it won't bring his grade point average down. Dr. Fleishman, the counselor, says he'd be happy to monitor the new arrangement and will seek additional help for Braxton if he has any further problems with the subject after the teacher does his part.

Jayne got what she wanted because she went through the proper channels, first consulting the assistant principal and counselor to get find an answer. More important, she explained the problem briefly to the teacher using the magic words "I hope you can help us."

HELP YOUR CHILD TALK TO THE TEACHER ABOUT A POOR GRADE

Ms. Brookins, the parent of a middle school student, called Ms. Morgan, her daughter Chantel's English teacher, regarding what the teacher considered her rude behavior after receiving a D grade in English.

As Ms. Morgan tells it, Chantel stormed into her teacher's classroom while she was teaching a class, slammed her backpack on the teacher's desk, and screamed, "Why did you give me a lousy grade? I don't deserve this."

Because of Chantel's loud outburst and the class disruption, Ms. Morgan wrote a pink slip and asked the dean to give Chantel a one-day in-school suspension and required that her parent come to school to reinstate her. When Chantel got home, she complained that the teacher was unfair to punish her that way in addition to giving her a poor grade.

Ms. Brookins listened to what her daughter said then paused a moment so that her daughter could process the full impact of what happened and so that she could read the disapproval of her actions on her mother's face. Chantel asked her mother what she could do to fix the problem. "After you serve your in-school suspension, I'll come in to reinstate you, and then you'll tell your teacher you're sorry for barging into her class and screaming at her about your grade."

Chantel protested that it was the teacher who was wrong in giving her a poor grade because she always participated in class and did her homework. Ms. Brookins told her that if she wanted to improve her grade next time, she should ask her teacher how much participation and homework counted in her grade.

After Chantel served her suspension, she and her mother appeared at the dean of discipline's office for her reinstatement. They waited until Ms. Morgan, the English teacher, had a free period. After Chantel asked her how much class participation and homework assignments counted, she told her and her mother that she had explained all that clearly at the beginning of the year.

The teacher reiterated that tests counted for 75 percent and that class participation and homework carried a 25 percent weight in her total average. Chantel apologized to Ms. Morgan for her outburst; Ms. Morgan, in turn, graciously accepted Chantel's apology for interrupting her class and making a scene about her poor grade. She also offered to help tutor Chantel on a weekly basis and recommended a student tutor from the volunteer peer tutoring center at the school.

After thinking about it, Chantel realized that she'd acted rashly in her approach to complaining about her grade. When mother and daughter finished meeting with the teacher, Ms. Brookins reminded Chantel that there's a better way to approach a teacher when you get a bad grade. As a follow up, she asked Chantel to give her some ideas for how she could phrase her concerns if she ever received a poor grade in the future.

After Chantel thought about it over dinner, she wrote out some answers to her mother's question about how to approach a teacher more effectively in the future. Here are some statements Chantel came up with: "I was surprised and upset to get that grade in your class. Can you give me some ideas so I can do better next report period?"; "I want to improve my grade next time. Can we have a conference so I can get some suggestions about how to do that?"; and "How can you help me improve my grade next time? What should I concentrate on to improve?"

Chantel worked hard to raise her English grade, and with Ms. Morgan's help, she earned a C+ for the second report period. She's hoping for a B next time.

ASK THE PRINCIPAL TO MINIMIZE CLASSROOM INTERRUPTIONS

Lately, the teaching staff at a local high school has experienced many interruptions from the PA system that have cut into instructional time. The teacher's union representative, with the advice and consent of the other five teachers on the school union committee, brought this problem to the principal's attention in a closed-door meeting. The principal explained that she wanted to interest the students in upcoming school events, such as sports, drama, and spirit night, and that making these announcements was the only way to inform the entire student body. Signs posted in the hallway didn't work as well as talking directly to the students via the PA system.

The teachers' union representative said that many teachers complained that the principal's announcements interrupted classes at inopportune times, such as when a teacher gives instructions for an important test or tries to explain a difficult concept to the class.

In asking the principal to refrain from interrupting classes too often with his messages, the union representative told her that he appreciated the fact that the principal wanted to generate excitement among the students about upcoming events but that teachers were becoming frustrated about the frequent interruptions. Did she have any ideas about how to deliver the announcements without intruding upon instructional time?

The principal countered that she could make some of the announcements during homeroom when all students were present. She could also ask the student council, teams, and clubs to post their flyers and posters about their events in strategic places in the halls and lunchroom. She also agreed to make congratulatory announcements to students about academic and athletic achievements during assemblies.

While the principal agreed to seek alternatives to delivering the announcements when students were in class, she also said that sometimes when things come up at the last minute, she might have to make an exception and interrupt the class.

While the union representative agreed that exceptions might arise, he said that he'd like to meet with the other teachers in the teachers' union committee so that they could agree upon how they'd limit these emergency announcements so they didn't occur too often. The principal emphasized that she'd like to hear their ideas and would also like her input taken into consideration.

The union representative thanked the principal for listening to the committee's concerns and said he looked forward to discussing the issue further before the union committee met to exchange ideas for dealing with emergency announcements by answering the following questions: What constitutes an emergency announcement? How often should an administrator be able to interrupt the class for such an announcement? What alternatives could they give the principal for interrupting classes?

The union representative was polite in his meeting with the principal and gave her a chance to voice her concerns about the issue. He started off on a positive note when he praised the principal by saying that he appreciated how she wanted to create a climate of enthusiasm for upcoming events. He also requested a follow-up meeting in which the entire faculty would present their ideas to the principal so that they could come to a consensus about dealing with the issue of class interruptions and also consider how to handle emergency announcements that might come up.

Due to the representative's concern and willingness to get both sides to compromise, the administration and the union reached a settlement that satisfied both parties.

HELP YOUR CHILD SUCCEED IN SCHOOL BY ASKING THE RIGHT QUESTIONS

Another school year is about to start for Aiden, who barely passed ninth grade last year. His parents, Mr. and Mrs. Tyson, want to be sure he's off to a good start. Mrs. Tyson called the school to see if Aiden could see his counselor, Ms. Williams, before school starts to map out a plan for his success as a tenth grader. The counselor made an appointment to speak with Aiden and his parents about their concerns for the coming year. Aiden's main problems deal with trying to figure out teachers' expectations of him and how to ask for help with school issues if he needs it.

Here is a conversation the family had with the school counselor, asking questions to ensure Aiden's academic success and inquiring about assistance from his teachers if he needs it.

Ms. Williams: I'm glad you came in with Aiden, Mr. and Mrs. Tyson. It will help reinforce some tips for success I'd like him to consider.

Ms. Williams (addressing Aiden): The first thing you need to do in all your classes, Aiden, is listen carefully the first couple days of class to what the teacher expects of you. Each one of your teachers will clearly lay out a plan to help you get the grades you want. They'll give you a handout that lists their requirements for the course and explains how they'll figure out your report card grade. They'll factor in your class-work, participation, homework, and mainly tests. Take careful notes when your teachers give their course expectations.

Aiden: I can do that. But sometimes they don't make it clear, and I don't understand what they want from me.

Ms. Williams: Then it's your job to be curious and ask them questions the first few days of school.

Mrs. Tyson: If you can't understand something as the year goes on, keep asking questions. That's the most important way you'll know how to perform well in their classes.

Ms. Williams: I agree, Mrs. Tyson. Keep that curiosity going, and don't hesitate to ask questions throughout the year. Your teachers are there to help and want you to do well. Aiden, can you think of any questions you may want to ask if the teacher hasn't mentioned them the first few days of school?

Aiden: These would be ones I'd like to know: What types of tests do you usually give, such as true/false, multiple choice, or group pro-jects? How much does class participation count?

Mr. Tyson: Suppose you got some grades you weren't happy about, like you did last year. What would you say to the teacher?

Aiden (smiling): You wouldn't be asking that because I messed up when I talked to my math teacher about my grade last year, would you?

Mr. Tyson: As a matter of fact, after you talked to her, things got worse between you. I remember that well. So, how could you find a better way to ask how you could improve your grade?

Aiden: I remember that I was angry because I knew you would ground me; I took my anger out on the teacher when I saw her in a conference. Things went downhill, and I said, "You don't know how to teach. That's why I flunked your class." She said that saying mean stuff to her wasn't going to help me do better next time.

Mrs. Tyson: What would you say if this happened again in one of your classes?

Aiden: I'd take a tip from my counselor and say something like, "I want to do better in your class. Tell me what I have to do to pass next time," and I'd write down what the teacher said.

Ms. Williams: That sounds more reasonable. If you or your parents have any other questions about how to talk to your teachers about having a better year than last year, I'm here for you.

After Aiden and his parents spoke with Ms. Williams, they felt better about the plan to help him improve. He followed their advice and took notes the first few days of class about what his teachers expected of him. If a problem came up, he spoke to his teachers courteously when he asked them to help him come up with a plan to improve in their classes. In the end, a little bit of planning and a lot of tact went a long way because Aiden passed all his classes the first semester of tenth grade.

ASK FOR THE SCHOOL BOARD'S HELP

When you believe you have no further recourse as a parent with a problem involving your child's school experience, as a last resort, turn to your local school board for help. They're elected community members who represent you and will help you solve your problem.

A group of four parents complained to the elementary school principal that their children had to walk on dangerous roads to the bus stop because the school district did not allow busing if the children lived less than a mile from the school. The school buses in the area that were passing through the main thoroughfare where the students walked to school could not stop to pick up the students because of the district rule. The principal referred the parents to the school district transportation department that immediately said the rule couldn't be altered.

The parents did not want to give up ensuring their children a safe ride to school. They called the school superintendent, who upheld the district ruling that said their children were not entitled to busing because they lived too close to the school. Although the parents emphasized how fast, unsafe traffic precluded their children walking safely to school, the superintendent said he couldn't do anything to change the rule. What should be the parents' next step? They knew they had to do something.

One of the parents, a paralegal, said that it wouldn't hurt to try one more agency to help them win their case. The next day the parents drew up a petition and asked a school board member who seemed sympathetic to their plight to help them. The school board member accepted their petition and said he'd see what he could do to assist them.

He spoke to the superintendent, who told him the same thing he told the parents, that they could not change the busing rule that had been in place for years. The school board member took it upon himself to call the state Department of Transportation for schools and asked them to reconsider the rule. The Department of Transportation representative got back to the school board member immediately. She said that since the buses on that route wouldn't be going out of the way, she would give permission for the buses to stop for the four students involved and transport them to their school.

The school board voted unanimously on the resolution and subsequently implemented a district-wide rule stating that buses would be allowed to stop for students if the bus was already passing through that area.

In this case, the parents had to ask the principal, the school superintendent, and finally a school board member for help. The spokesperson for the parents, a parent himself, always made his requests brief and polite. He used wording such as "I need you to help me get busing for our children. The route they take in walking to their elementary school is unsafe." When talking to the various authorities, the spokesperson used assertive speech and body language.

The parties to whom the parents spoke listened and responded quickly to what the spokesperson and other parents who accompanied him said. The spokesperson worked his way through the channels in a systematic way, ending at the school board member, who understood the problem and empathized with him because he had children and wouldn't want them to walk with dangerous traffic facing them on their trip to school each day.

If the parents hadn't asked and had just accepted the school district busing rule, they would not have accomplished the task of ensuring a safe bus ride for their children. They went through the proper channels, stated their problem clearly, and persisted until they got exactly what they wanted.

In all the anecdotes in this book, those who asked someone for something took control of the situation, believed they had the upper hand, and invariably got what they wanted. If you use the techniques in this book and persist, you will too.

INSTANT REVIEW

Chapter 10: Ask and Receive in the Educational Arena

- Know the right person to ask.
- Ask for books, equipment, and supplies.
- Request help for a problem with your child's teacher.
- Help your child discuss a poor grade with the teacher.
- Ask the principal to minimize class interruptions.
- Help your child succeed in school by asking the right questions.
- Ask for the school board's help when you need it.

11

THINK ABOUT HOW TO ASK HARD QUESTIONS

Here are some commonly asked hard questions about how to ask for something you want and advice about how to say no when someone asks you for something that you don't want to give. See if they match any of your concerns. If you have a question similar to the ones listed here, think about what you would say. You may want to pattern your response on one stated here, using your own words and personality to generate an answer that's right for you.

Q. *I feel that I'm imposing by asking people to do things for me, but I sometimes need help. I can't walk well because of a bad knee. Lifting heavy things presents a big problem if I go grocery shopping, but I feel uncomfortable asking for help.*
A. Most people are more than willing to help but may not know something is wrong unless you ask. If you're in a store, you could say to a worker, "I'm hoping you can help me by loading these groceries into my cart. I'd appreciate it if you'd pack them lightly. My knee's bothering me, and it's hard to lift heavy things." The checker will gladly help you and will also ask another employee to take your groceries to the car.

Q. *My church wants me to ask my friends to contribute toward a holiday gift fund for needy families. I know it's a good cause, but I hate bothering people for money. What's the best way to ask without getting on people's nerves?*

A. I can understand your reluctance to solicit money, even for what you consider a worthy cause. Simply say, "Would you be willing to contribute to a holiday fund my church is sponsoring for families in need?" Then see what the people say. If they decline, at least you've asked. If they say yes, they may want to know what the average gift is; you can discuss this with your organization ahead of time so you have an answer.

Q. *My mother-in-law is always asking me to go shopping or out to lunch with her, but frankly, I don't enjoy her company and would rather do something else during my rare free time. How can I say no without getting on her wrong side?*
A. Tell her you're very busy and have little time to shop or go out to lunch (it's the truth), but give her a specific time you'd be able to spend a reasonable amount of time with her doing what she likes on an occasional basis. Say something like this: "Sorry, I'm not free for a while, but if you'd like, I have a little time in a couple of weeks on a Monday. Would you like to meet at [pick a place that's quick] for lunch?" There's no need for long explanations when you don't want to do something. The person who's asking for your company may get suspicious if you talk too much. The less said, the better, works in most cases whether you're asking or answering.

Q. *I have a nosy neighbor who asks personal questions that I don't want to answer (How old are you? How much did you pay for your outfit? What medicines do you take?). How can I ask her to stop asking personal questions without seeming rude?*
A. Don't worry about seeming rude when your neighbor is the one who asked these questions. Smile politely, and tell her you don't feel comfortable answering her questions. You could use Dear Abby's line: "Why do you want to know that?" while giving her an incredulous look. These replies should suffice with any busybody.

Q. *How can I ask my child's social studies teacher to stop picking on him because he doesn't participate in class? He's a quiet kid who doesn't like to stand out in a group. It's painful for him to talk in public, let alone volunteer in class.*
A. If you phrase it to make it sound like the teacher is picking on him, the teacher may take offense. Make an appointment to see the teacher (with-

out your child), and let him know that your child feels that he singles him out for not participating. Here's what you can say: "I'm concerned because Trey thinks you single him out for not participating in class. He's a shy child and doesn't like to speak up. I want to let you know so that maybe you can cut him some slack and help him feel more at ease with you and the students before expecting him to speak out in your class. What do you suggest?"

It's important to tell the teacher the problem without alienating him and also to propose a solution. In most cases, you'll find a common ground to help your child.

Q. *There are two families living in the condo next door to me. They frequently have wild, noisy parties and keep my family and me awake on the weekends. I don't want to involve the police since I have to live near them and don't plan to move in the near future. How can I get them to stop?*

A. It's best not to knock on their door or enter their home because you don't know how they'll react. Say what you have to in public, preferably with a witness present. When you see one of the adults outside, speak to her calmly. Tell her that you need her and the other people living in the house to keep the noise down when they have parties. Wait for a response. If it's not a positive one, say you'll have to use other measures if a compromise isn't forthcoming.

Try to solve the problem on your own. Escalating it often proves more disruptive. You can try calling your neighborhood association if you have one or your condo manager. If nothing else works, take up the matter with the local police, who will first try to mediate the problem before escalating it.

Q. *My sister borrowed a large sum of money from me for a down payment on a house. She promised to pay me back within six months. Now a year has gone by. I had her sign a contract that we drew up together. I've asked for the money a couple of times as I need it to pay my bills, which have increased since my son started college. I offered to put her on an installment plan to pay me back, but she says she doesn't have any money to spare. I don't think she'll ever pay me back. What should I say to get her to pay?*

A. Give her one more chance. Appeal to her sense of fairness. You might say, "I need the money I loaned you now as I have added expenses with Colin starting college this year. Let's draw up a plan right now that we can easily live with."

If she continues to protest that she doesn't have the money, take a tough stance and say, "I can't wait any longer for the money I loaned you. You signed a contract, and if I don't get the money, we'll settle it through small-claims court. I don't want to ruin our relationship, but I've waited long enough. If you don't have the money, you can borrow it from the bank, but I need you to pay me back in a month."

Don't back down. Your sister will find a way if she wants to. What she's doing is a deal breaker.

Q. *I work with computers in my job, and my neighbor is always asking me to come over and address his computer issues. I try to help him when I have time, but lately it's getting to be an imposition. I have to take care of my house and pets after working all day and need time to rest. How can I say no without alienating him as a neighbor?*
A. There will always be people who will take advantage of your good nature and willingness to help them. If this person is calling on you too often and imposing on your free time, speak up, or you'll always be at his beck and call and resent him.

The next time he asks, say: "Lately, you've called on me a lot, sometimes to the point that I have to delay something I need to do around the house to drop everything to fix your computer. I'm willing to help in an emergency, but only occasionally, as I'm very busy. I'll give you the names of a couple of people you can call who fix computers for a fee if your computer company can't help."

Do not let yourself be used or abused. Always set the conditions upon which you'll help a friend or family member.

Q. *My friend from college loves my clothes and jewelry and often asks to borrow them for a special occasion, like a wedding. She makes more as a beauty consultant than I do as a newspaper reporter, but she thinks nothing of asking to borrow my things. The truth is that I don't like other people wearing my clothes and jewelry, not that I'm a germaphobe, but I like to keep them in perfect shape and ready to wear for my own special* *occasions. Am I being selfish? If not, what do I say to her the next time she asks to borrow something?*

A. Saying no is sometimes harder than asking for something. Most people would think it's presumptuous of your friend to ask to borrow your favorite clothes and jewelry on a regular basis. You're not being selfish because you don't want to give in to her every wish. Tell her that your clothes and jewelry are special possessions and that you don't feel comfortable lending them out. If she's a friend, she'll understand. If not, maybe you need to reevaluate your friendship.

Q. *Recently, I've experienced leaking from my bladder. I can't control it so that I can get to the bathroom in time. I find it hard to discuss what I consider embarrassing health problems with my doctor. How can I ask for help if I feel awkward bringing up the question?*

A. Your doctor has heard of this and any other problem you've experienced. Say, "I feel awkward telling you this, but I've had a problem with urine leaking, and I can't seem to control it. Do you have any ideas to help solve my problem?" Your doctor will be happy to provide you with a solution that's right for you.

Q. *I suffer from depression but am leery of discussing it with family or close friends because I don't want them to worry about me or to perceive me as weak. How can I bring up the subject? No one would ever guess I'm depressed because I'm always the one that's there for everyone when they need me.*

A. The most important thing in curing mental illness is to be able to talk about it, which isn't always easy. First, choose someone with whom you feel totally at ease, a person who you don't think will judge you or give you unsolicited advice. It could be a friend, family member, or medical professional. If you don't want to talk to any of these people, call a mental health hotline. They'll give you information about organizations you can call to get immediate assistance.

If you're talking to a trusted friend or family member, say something like this: "I'm not sure if you've noticed, but things aren't going well for me. I've been feeling down for a while, and I have to push myself to work and take care of the kids. Have you ever felt that way, and, if so, what helped in your case?"

If you don't get any answers from the person you ask, seek help from a medical professional, or call a mental health hotline. Google "mental health hotlines in my area" to find one you can call.

Q. *I sent out invitations to my wife's sixtieth birthday party to be held at an upscale restaurant. Four people haven't yet responded, and I need to get a total count of everyone attending in a week. I've tried calling and texting, but I can't reach these people.*

A. Although basic etiquette requires people to respond in a timely manner to invitations, some people forget, and others don't take RSVPs seriously. If you reach the person, say this: "Hopefully, you got my invitation to my wife's birthday party at the Ritz next week. I haven't heard from you. I need to know if you and your husband will attend so that I can give the hall an accurate count. Will you be able to make it?"

If you've tried all methods of contacting nonresponders and can't reach them, contact one of their close friends or family members to let them know you've attempted to get in touch with these people and that you need a response by the end of the week. If you still can't get an answer, consider them no-shows.

Q. *I've been friends with someone since high school and have lived in the same neighborhood for years. A few years ago after much scrimping and saving, I acquired a shore house. My longtime friend loves the shore and feels free to visit me every summer despite the fact that I've told her I usually have children and grandchildren visiting regularly. This year she gave me a day's notice, and I scrambled to get my home in order to accommodate her. She's already overstayed her weekly visit by three days and says she's having such a great time she wants to spend the rest of the week at my cottage. What do I say to get her to leave?*

A. You said your family visits frequently. You must miss having time to yourself to sunbathe on the beach and walk the boardwalk at night. The last thing you want is to feel obligated to run a guesthouse on your visitor's terms. Here's how you can phrase it when you talk to this free-loader: "I know you're enjoying your stay, but I've planned to spend the next few days alone working on my projects. We can get together for a couple of days next year, but I'll have to check my schedule first to find a good time."

You don't need to explain any further. She's the one who's imposing. If she doesn't return next year, you'll find yourself with even more free time. Who needs a friend who's a moocher?

Q. *An acquaintance at my gym keeps asking me to hang out, one day for breakfast at the Pancake House, the next for a few beers at the local watering hole. I have little free time in my busy schedule as a sales manager at a car dealership, and I prefer to spend what free time I have with close friends I've made over the years. I feel like I don't have anything in common with this person, other than my gym membership.*
A. Here's what to say: "Thanks for your invitation, but I'm busy day and night and don't have much free time for a social life. This is my only recreation. I hope you understand." That should give him the message that pancakes and beer are out of the question, at least with him.

Q. *A conference attendee where I gave a talk about selling my writing sent an email to my website, asking if she could contact me with a question about writing. After I graciously agreed, she wrote that she'd like to meet with me to "pick your brain" about potential publishers for her romance novel. I know it will take a lot of time that I don't have, between my writing business and my family obligations. What do I tell her?*
A. Simple. Here's what to say: "I appreciate your taking the time to attend my talk. I have to limit myself to paying customers to meet and discuss potential publishers for their writing. Let me know if you're interested in setting up a phone conversation about my services or if you'd like me to email information. Thanks for your interest."

Q. *I'm a senior widow who met an interesting guy at a local diner; we had a pleasant conversation about theater, our mutual interest. I know he goes to this eatery at least once a week. How can I ask him for a date? Although most of us are liberated by now, it still feels a little awkward for me to ask as I was raised back in the day when guys usually did the asking.*
A. There's no need to feel awkward as ladies are as likely to ask for a date as men these days. The next time you see him at the diner, after engaging in small talk, say this: "I see we're both theater buffs. There's a play you may be interested in at the Walnut Street Theater next week. I wonder if

you'd like to go with me. We could grab a bite here afterward if you'd like."

Wait for a response, and go from there. That was easy—right?

Q. *Last year my cousin went to an auto license center to renew her license. Everyone was crowded into benches waiting for the receptionist to call them. The lady my cousin sat next to saw her reading a book about using intuition to solve problems. They struck up a conversation about metaphysics; my cousin's seatmate said that these tools to sharpen your intuition were an instrument of the devil that would subject her to the fires of hell.*

When my cousin, who is a professional psychic medium, disagreed, the lady invited her to come to her church to be saved. She proceeded to give my cousin a long sermon. My cousin didn't want to be impolite, so she ended up an unwilling captive, listening to this self-proclaimed preacher for half an hour. Luckily, the receptionist finally told my cousin it was her turn to take her license picture. What could my cousin have said to shorten the time she spent with this intrusive woman?

A. No one can be a captive unless she lets herself be one. As soon as the woman sitting next to your cousin started giving her unwanted opinions, your cousin could have said, with strong eye contact and in a firm voice, "This conversation is over" or "I don't want [or need] to hear this," and immediately changed her seat.

Q. *Men frequently ask my friend Tiara out on dates as she's intelligent and elegant. If she finds one of these prospects attractive and has vetted him by talking to friends who know him, she's often willing to give him a chance. Recently, Andre, a young man she knows from her law firm, asked her out to dinner. She likes him as a friend and respects him as a colleague but has no romantic interest in him as she thinks he's too serious and somewhat pompous, definitely not her type. How can she tell him that she doesn't want to make that date without hurting his feelings?*

A. Here's what your friend can say to Andre: "Thanks for asking me out, but for now, I'd like to keep our relationship the way it is—as friends. I don't want anything to get in the way of that, so dating probably wouldn't work." If he protests, she can say, "That's the way I feel at this time, so it has to be that way. We can leave things open for a later time and reevaluate how we feel about it."

Q. *A restaurant I love makes the best lemon chiffon dessert with a secret topping. I'd love to make it at home, but the hostess refuses to divulge the recipe as it's been in the family for fifty years. What can I do to get the recipe?*

A. Do you know of someone else in the restaurant who will divulge it? I once frequented a restaurant where the hostess's granddaughter was a server. Unlike her grandmother, who was distant and unyielding, Hannah said yes to my request and wrote out the recipe.

If the hostess doesn't have any family members, like the granddaughter, working in the restaurant, you might try this: "I've told you how much we love your lemon chiffon dessert. I know it's a family heirloom, and I respect your right to keep it a secret, but if you could see it in your heart to give it to me, I'd be forever grateful."

* * *

Here's the recipe for lemon chiffon dessert that I adapted to make it more user friendly.

LEMON CHIFFON DESSERT

Ingredients for Crust for 13 x 9 x 2 Pan

Softened butter for greasing pan
1½ cups graham cracker crumbs, finely crushed
¼ cup granulated or brown sugar (I prefer brown)
½ cup butter, melted

Instructions

Grease 13x9x2 pan lightly with softened butter. Combine next 3 ingredients; press graham cracker mixture onto bottom and sides of pan. Chill in refrigerator.

Ingredients for Lemon Filling

1 12-oz can regular evaporated milk (not low fat)

1 3-oz package lemon Jell-O gelatin (not lemon pudding)
1¾ cups boiling water
¼ cup real lemon juice (not processed)
1 cup granulated sugar

Instructions

1. Chill unopened can of evaporated milk in refrigerator overnight.
2. Dissolve Jell-O in boiling water and chill until partially set. Whip until light and fluffy.
3. Add lemon juice and sugar.
4. Whip the chilled evaporated milk and fold into Jell-O mixture.
5. Pour mixture into crust that has been chilled. Pour slowly so you don't move the crumbs.
6. Chill until set, about six or more hours. Check to see when it's hard enough to cut.
7. Sprinkle on cake topping (see below).

For Cake Topping

Ten or more (more is better) vanilla wafer cookies with vanilla cream cookies (not plain vanilla wafers). Voortman makes these cookies. They have a layer of vanilla cream in the middle. Sprinkle these chopped cookies (chop them coarsely in a food processor) on the cake after you chill it. Serve dessert plain or with whipped cream.

OTHER BOOKS BY THE AUTHOR

101 Ways to Help Preschoolers Excel in Reading, Writing, and Speaking (2007)
Real Life Bully Prevention for Real Kids: 50 Ways to Help Elementary and Middle School Students (2009)
Who Says Bullies Rule? Common Sense Tips to Help Your Kids Cope (2011)
Excuse Me, Your Participle's Dangling: How to Use Grammar to Make Your Writing Powers Soar (2013)
Cool Things to Do If a Bully's Bugging You: 50 Classroom Activities to Help Elementary Students (2016)
Helping Kids Live Mindfully: A Grab Bag of Classroom Activities for Middle School Students (2017)
Parenting Mindfully: 101 Ways to Help Raise Caring and Responsible Kids in an Unpredictable World (2018)

ABOUT THE AUTHOR

Catherine DePino has written twenty books about bullying, grammar/ writing, spirituality, and women's issues. She recently published *Parenting Mindfully: 101 Ways to Help Raise Caring and Responsible Kids in an Unpredictable World*. Her self-help book, *Fire Up Your Life in Retirement: 101 Ways for Women to Reinvent Themselves*, helps women deal with the challenges they face in retirement. Her bully prevention book, *Blue Cheese Breath and Stinky Feet: How to Deal with Bullies*, was published in many different languages. Bully prevention programs value it as a treasured resource. She also wrote *Helping Kids Live Mindfully: A Grab Bag of Activities for Middle School Students.*

Her background includes a BS in English and Spanish education, a master's in English education, and a doctorate in curriculum theory and development and educational administration with principal's certification, all from Temple University.

The author worked for thirty-one years as a teacher, department head, and disciplinarian in the Philadelphia School District. After this, she worked at Temple as an adjunct assistant professor and student teaching supervisor.

Catherine has also written articles for national magazines, including the *Christian Science Monitor* and the *Writer*. She views her most important accomplishment in life as being the mother of three children and the grandmother of five.

For many years, she served on the board of the Philadelphia Writers' Conference and has acted as a manuscript judge and speaker. Visit her website at www.catherinedepino.com.